# RING OF TRUTH

—serendipity <u>45</u>

— an example of memory's
retentive powers in
less sophisticated cultures — <u>61</u>

<u>89</u> — CSLewis appeared to me, after his
death

# RING OF TRUTH

*A Translator's Testimony*

*by*

## J. B. PHILLIPS

**HODDER AND STOUGHTON**

Copyright © 1967 by J. B. Phillips
First published 1967
Sixth impression 1969

SBN 340 02343 0

Printed in Great Britain for Hodder and Stoughton Limited,
St. Paul's House, Warwick Lane, London, E.C.4, by
Cox & Wyman Limited, London, Reading and Fakenham

## Acknowledgments

I feel I must record my gratitude to all the people, young and old, who have written to me from many parts of the world. They, and the many friends with whom I have had personal conversations and discussions have helped and encouraged me, possibly without knowing it, to write this short book. I think it is those who have borne suffering with radiant faith who have above all renewed and deepened my own convictions.

To all these people it seems only fair to me to record my heartfelt gratitude.

I am also grateful to the Editor of the *Church Times* for permission to quote the letter on pp. 87–8.

Swanage, Dorset                                              J. B. PHILLIPS

# FOREWORD

I DO NOT write for scholars; they can look after themselves. For twenty-five years I have written for the ordinary man who is no theologian. Alas, today, he frequently gets the impression that the New Testament is no longer historically reliable.

What triggered off my anger (righteous, I trust) against some of our "experts" is this. A clergyman, old, retired, useless if you like, took his own life because his reading of the "new theology" and even some programmes on television, finally drove him, in his loneliness and ill-health, to conclude that his own life's work had been founded upon a lie. He felt that these highly-qualified writers and speakers must know so much more than he that they must be right. Jesus Christ did not really rise from the dead and the New Testament, on which he had based his life and ministry, was no more than a bundle of myths.

That made me angry, and I remembered the terrible words of Jesus which, in effect, say that a man would be better off dead than cause one of "his little ones to stumble". For many years it has been my solid purpose to communicate the truth of the Christian Gospel. I am *not* concerned to distort or dilute the Christian faith so that modern undergraduates, for example, can accept it without a murmur. I am concerned with the truth revealed in and through Jesus Christ. Let the modern world conform to him, and never let us dare to try to make him fit into our clever-clever modern world. I am no anti-intellectual, any more than St. Paul, who wrote so penetratingly that "the world by wisdom knew not God". But I say quite bluntly that some of the intellectuals (by no means all, thank God!), who write so cleverly and devastatingly about the Christian faith appear to have no personal knowledge of the living God. For they lack awe, they lack humility, and they lack the responsibility which every Christian owes to his weaker brother. They make sure they are never made "fools for Christ's sake", however many people's faith they may undermine.

Few people have had such a close and constant contact with the New Testament as I have. Even fewer have taken the trouble to understand the business of "communication". I say this in no spirit of conceit; it is a matter of simple fact. I therefore felt that it was high time that someone, who has spent the best years of his life in studying both the New Testament and good modern communicative English, spoke out. I do not care a rap what the *"avant-garde"* scholars say; I do very much care what God says and does. I have therefore felt compelled to write this book. It is my testimony to the historicity and reliability of the New Testament.

J. B. PHILLIPS

In a recent book* the Revd. Harry Williams, Dean of Trinity College, Cambridge, draws attention to the two kinds of truth which face us as human beings. One is the "outside" sort, which means the knowledge of ascertained facts in whatever department of human activity we are involved but which is outside our own personalities. The other kind of truth to which Mr. Williams draws our attention is the "inside" truth. This is the truth we know within ourselves, in part intuitively and in part as a result of experience. It grows out of fear, disappointment and doubt as well as out of joy, conviction and confident faith. Indeed Mr. Wiliams goes so far as to suggest, tentatively at least, that there might be a kind of theology of this inner self.

I believe that such a "theology" might answer several very important questions. What is it, for example, that lives within the spirit of a man which enables him to detect truth, even though it may prove painful and destructive to his previous illusions? Here lies one of life's great mysteries. What God-given faculty is it that enables us to recognise the Word of God as the Word of God and not as a mere human opinion or doctrine? Of course the moment we accept the Christian belief that all men are, at least potentially, the sons of God there is at least the beginning of an explanation. Why should not the son recognise, however faintly, the true tone of his Father's voice?

From my own experience, that is from my own knowledge of my own inner truth, I believe this recognition of God's word to be a valid part of human experience. And

* *The True Wilderness* (Constable).

when I find, as I have done over the last thirty years, that this inner experience is shared by thousands in various parts of the world, I am convinced that here is an authentic part of human existence which is all too often ignored. It is not so much that the bare Word speaks to us from the New Testament out of context (although, of course, it sometimes does that), as that what God has to say through the inspired writers sheds a quite unique light upon human living and dying.

## THE POWER OF THE WORD

I have said that the bare Word sometimes speaks to a man quite out of context, and that fact can be verified from the records of the Bible Society. Without any human intermediary a Gospel or even a verse from a Gospel can speak to any man reading it in his own tongue for the first time. The result is not infrequently dramatic: a man's whole attitude to life may be changed. God has spoken to him and he is (in the New Testament sense) converted. I cannot give individual examples without breaking confidences, but I have plenty of evidence in my files of this kind of thing. I am not thinking of people whose upbringing was steeped in biblical teaching and who then, after years of rebellion and evasion, were challenged by being confronted by a truth which was in fact part of their childhood's training. Of course that does happen, but I am thinking of men and women of various nationalities who had no Christian indoctrination in their early years and had never read the New Testament in their lives before. Yet their way of living was altered fundamentally when God spoke to them through these writings.

But having said this, it does not seem to me a common thing for a mere "text" to challenge, still less convert, anyone. Yet a close study of the remarkable collection of books which are known as the New Testament can, and constantly does, challenge, provoke and appeal to a man at a deeper level and with a more profound authority than any other human writing. Human beings can easily insulate themselves from any shock or disturbance of this kind by simply not reading it. So long as a man confines his ideas of Christ to a rather misty hero-figure of long ago who died a tragic death, and so long as his ideas of Christianity are bounded by what he calls the Sermon on the Mount (which he has almost certainly not read in its entirety since he became grown-up), then the living truth never has a chance to touch him. This is plainly what has happened to many otherwise intelligent people. Over the years I have had hundreds of conversations with people, many of them of higher intellectual calibre than my own, who quite obviously had no idea of what Christianity is really about. I was in no case trying to catch them out; I was simply and gently trying to find out what they knew about the New Testament. My conclusion was that they knew virtually nothing. This I find pathetic and somewhat horrifying. It means that the most important Event in human history is politely and quietly by-passed. For it is not as though the evidence had been examined and found unconvincing; it had simply never been examined.

Apart from sheer neglect, the other way in which human beings can protect themselves from the rather frightening vitality of the New Testament is by carefully dismembering it. It is obviously right that we should have

New Testament scholars – indeed I owe much to them – but it is horribly possible so to dissect your subject that you remove its life. By the time each source and component has been tagged and labelled this vibrant and compelling body of writing is no more than a cadaver on the theological operating-table.

## THE EXPERTS' RESPONSIBILITY

Although I know personally several excellent New Testament scholars who would certainly regard the material of their study with the utmost reverence, it is worth pointing out how criticisms by experts percolate through to the non-expert as detrimental and destructive. Perhaps this is unavoidable in our modern society, but I cannot forget Christ's stern words about "causing one of his little ones to stumble", or Paul's warning about "the weaker brother". We who have grown into a strong and mature faith must surely regard it as part of our responsibility to do or say nothing which would undermine faith. I believe this to be especially binding upon us in the fields of mass communication. What can profitably be discussed between men of many years' Christian experience may be quite unsuitable for a television programme, which may be seen by the weak, the fearful, the lonely and the dying. I make no plea for obscurantism. Those who know me as a parish priest will agree that I have always taken the line that if the Christian faith can be destroyed by somebody or other's clever-clever talk it cannot be basically very strong. But the broadcaster, and perhaps especially the solo television speaker, enjoys an almost *ex cathedra* position of non-contradiction. I am convinced that he has no right to air his own doubts and fancies as though they were matters of agreed faith among Christians.

Various theological ideas have nowadays percolated through to ordinary people, and their effect has been to make them even less ready than before to read the New Testament with serious adult attention. Such phrases as "religion-less Christianity" are bandied about as though we had outgrown God. But if we read even the paperback *Letters and Papers from Prison* by the Christian martyr Dietrich Bonhoeffer, to whom the phrase is attributed, it is obvious that he did not mean anything of the kind. He was protesting, and rightly, against religion divorced from life – and what true Christian wouldn't? – but he was a deeply religious man to the day of his death. Nevertheless the phrase sticks. The modern humanist with his irrational prejudice against anything "supernatural" welcomes the idea of a sort of Christianity without religion. But, of course, true Christianity is rooted in both God and man. The New Testament gives no sort of endorsement to modern man's extraordinary illusion of being able to dispense with God.

## DE-MYTHOLOGISING

Further, we have the percolated influence of another German theologian, Rudolf Bultmann. His idea, which amounts to an obsession, is that "the life of Jesus is set in such a mythological framework that its real meaning can only be found when we get rid of the whole first century background".* I believe that this idea is almost wholly false. But what happens to the idea when it filters through

* Quoting William Neil, *The Life and Teaching of Jesus* (Hodder and Stoughton).

to the general people? Simply the impression that leading theologians and New Testament scholars all regard the stories of Jesus as "myths". And, make no mistake, that means to the ordinary man and woman that they are no more than concocted stories with about as much truth in them as the fables of Æsop and with about as much authority as the myth of Father Christmas. It would not be true to say that Bultmann and his very considerable following have any difficulty in combining their sceptical view of the historicity of the Gospels with a real devotion to the faith of the Church. But this demands an agility and dexterity which escapes me. All that I am concerned with is the effect of the Bultmann "de-mythologisation" upon ordinary non-theologically trained people.

## FIRST-HAND CONTACT

The New Testament, given a fair hearing, does not need me or anyone else to defend it. It has the proper ring for anyone who has not lost his ear for truth. But because in these days it has been compromised in the eyes of many people by those who should know better, I feel I can do no other than record my own impressions as honestly and faithfully as I can. As the years have passed – and it is now twenty-five years since I began translating the "Epistles" – my conviction has grown that the New Testament is in a quite special sense inspired. It is not magical, nor is it faultless: human beings wrote it. But by something which I would not hesitate to describe as a miracle, there is a concentration upon that area of inner truth which is fundamental and ageless. That, I believe, is the reason why millions of people have heard the voice of God speaking to them through these seemingly artless pages.

14

But before I begin my testimony as a translator I must make a few reservations. First, although I believe in the true inspiration of the New Testament and its obvious power to change human lives in this or any other century, I should like to make it quite clear that I could not possibly hold the extreme "fundamentalist" position of so-called "verbal inspiration". This theory is bound to break down sooner or later in the world of translation. There are over eleven hundred known human languages, and it was during a brief spell of work for the British and Foreign Bible Society that I learned of the attempts to translate the Bible, or at least parts of it, into nearly all of these different tongues. I learned of the extreme ingenuity which the translator must use to convey sense and truth where word-for-word transmission is out of the question. You cannot talk to tribes who live without ever seeing navigable water of our possessing "an anchor for the soul". You cannot speak to the Eskimos of "the Lamb of God which taketh away the sin of the world", or of Christ being "the true Vine" and of us, his disciples, as "the branches"! Such examples could, literally, be multiplied many thousands of times. Yet I have found, when addressing meetings in this country and in America, that there still survives a minority who passionately believe in verbal inspiration. It appears that they have never seriously thought that there are millions for whom Christ died who would find a word-for-word translation of the New Testament, even if it were possible, frequently meaningless. Any man who has sense as well as faith is bound to conclude that it is the *truths* which are inspired and not the words which are merely the vehicles of truth.

Secondly, although I have no wish to deny the great

truths embodied in that tremendous book of celestial poetry which we call the Book of Revelation, the general remarks which follow cannot be applied to that book. It is part of the New Testament, and I have no quarrel with those who included it in the sacred canon. I am only concerned here to say that it does stand in a special place and demands very special consideration.*

Thirdly, I had no intention of putting my version forward in some kind of competition with the beauty and majesty of the Authorised Version of 1611. I undertook the task of translation chiefly for the sake of the young people at that time under my care in wartime London. I suppose that like many another clergyman or minister I had never realised what a barrier beautiful but antique words had imposed.

## THE BEGINNING OF MY WORK

I began, then, with the Epistles, or Letters, of Paul. I felt that while most of the people to whom I was ministering had at least a nodding acquaintance with the Gospels, the Epistles were to them forbidding and "difficult". We were, like several millions in London, Christians in danger, and since much of the message of the New Testament Epistles is addressed to Christians in danger, I felt that here was an additional reason for putting them into English which could readily be understood.

It was not easy in those wartime days to set aside even a few hours a week for this work. I had very few books with me, and (as those who are old enough will remember) it was virtually impossible to get others – quite impossible if they were printed abroad. But I had a rare stroke of

* For those who are interested may I recommend my own Preface to *The Book of Revelation* (Bles or Fontana).

good fortune for which I am still grateful. I sent a copy of my version of "Colossians" (reprinted from a local Parish Magazine) to the late C. S. Lewis. He replied with great encouragement. He wrote – "It's like seeing an old picture after it's been cleaned", and that is a sentence which I remember and treasure, especially as that was precisely the effect I was trying to produce. A little later Lewis suggested that I should translate all the New Testament Epistles and it was he who suggested the excellent title, *Letters to Young Churches*.

### THE RELEASE OF TRUTH

The first effect of my work astonished me. The people for whom I had made this translation began to see, and sometimes saw quite suddenly, the relevance of these Letters to life. The removal of the old varnish allowed the truth to reach them in a way it had not reached them before. The second effect was upon me, the translator. I found, as I have written elsewhere, that once one gets to grips with the actual stuff of the New Testament, its vitality is astonishing. I found myself provoked, challenged, stimulated, comforted and generally convicted of my previous shallow knowledge of Holy Scripture. The centuries seemed to melt away and here was I confronted by eternal truths which my soul, however reluctantly, felt bound to accept. The further I went on with my work of translation the more this conviction of spiritual truth grew within me.

### – AND ITS ASTONISHING VITALITY

I must, in common justice, confess here that for years I had viewed the Greek of the New Testament with a rather snobbish disdain. I had read the best of Classical

Greek both at school and Cambridge for over ten years. To come down to the *Koine* of the first century A.D. seemed, as I have sometimes remarked rather uncharitably, like reading Shakespeare for some years and then turning to the Vicar's letter in the Parish Magazine! But I think now that I was wrong: I can see that the expression of the Word of God in ordinary workaday language is all of a piece with God's incredible humility in becoming Man in Jesus Christ. And, further, the language itself is not so pedestrian as I had at first supposed. Although I did my utmost to preserve an emotional detachment I found again and again that the material under my hands was strangely alive; it spoke to my condition in the most uncanny way. I say "uncanny" for want of a better word, but it was a very strange experience to sense, not occasionally but almost continually, the living quality of those rather strangely assorted books. To me it is the more remarkable because I had no fundamentalist upbringing, and although as a priest of the Anglican Church I had a great respect for Holy Scripture, this very close contact of several years of translation produced an effect of "inspiration" which I have never experienced, even in the remotest degree, in any other work.

## THE "OLD SCRIPTURE" BECAME NEW

I found this sense of inspiration highly communicable. Once the language difficulty was removed the Letters spoke for themselves. In the world of Paul, John, Peter and James we were in a world to many people as yet unexplored. The little stories of Jesus, half-remembered from Sunday School, and the unrealistic mental images which tender minds had absorbed of "Gentle Jesus meek and mild" were no longer appropriate. For the real world of the first century A.D. was tough and cruel, and the Christians who lived in it had to be real people, utterly convinced of their faith, utterly devoted to the Lord whom most of them had never seen. Their struggles, their endurance, their strength of purpose in the face of appalling odds seemed to us in those days of World War II to have an extraordinary relevance. The intervening centuries might never have been; inspired words took on a new and, so to speak, contemporary authority. Indeed so great was this sense of contemporaneity that we had constantly to remind ourselves of the different conditions of those early days: the danger and difficulties of travel, the uncertainties of communication and the lack of almost every modern "amenity". Further, there was a threat which loomed over these early Christian communities, the ever-present possibility of persecution and even of death. It is true that we were again and again threatened with death or mutilation by bombs from the German air force, but the sharing of common danger is not comparable with the persecution of a minority. Yet the spells of acute danger which we endured brought home to us the magnificent and joyful resilience of early Christianity. I can remember, for example, a particularly dangerous time, when we were officially urged not to have large groups of people assembled together. I used to conduct short services in people's houses or in air-raid shelters. Again and again passages from Paul's letters could scarcely have been more apt. One particular truth I tried to see then, and urged others to accept, is contained in Paul's words: "*in* all these things we are more than conquerors". (Rom.8: 37). We often think that eventually all will be well (and so it will), but Paul's point is that *in the midst* of cold and hunger, of danger to life and limb, we are more than conquerors.

When I started translating some of Paul's shorter letters I was at first alternately stimulated and annoyed by the outrageous certainty of his faith. It was not until I realised afresh what the man had actually achieved, and suffered, that I began to see that here was someone who was writing, not indeed at God's dictation, but by the inspiration of God himself. Sometimes you can see the conflicts between the pharisaic spirit of the former Saul (who could say such grudging things about marriage and insist upon the perennial submission of women), and the Spirit of God who inspired Paul to write that in Christ there is neither "Jew nor Greek . . . male nor female"!

Paul had, and still has, his detractors. There are those who say he is like the man who says "I don't want to boast, but—", and then proceeds to do that very thing! Very well then, but let us look at his list of "boasting". We have only to turn up 2 Corinthians 11: 23–27. Have any of us gone through a tenth of that catalogue of suffering and humiliation? Yet this is the man who can not only say that in all these things we are more than conquerors, but can also "reckon that the sufferings of this present time are not worthy to be compared with the glory which shall be revealed in us". (Rom. 8: 18). Here is no armchair philosopher, no ivory-tower scholar, but a man of almost incredible drive and courage, living out in actual human dangers and agonies the implications of his unswerving faith.

## PAUL'S LETTER TO CORINTH

But the Letter which really struck me a blow from which I have never recovered was the one popularly known as

"First Corinthians". Let me explain. I had been doing some background reading, and I was reminded that Corinth was a by-word, even in those wicked old days, for every kind of vice and depravity. The Greeks, as usual, had a word for it, and "to Corinthise yourself" was to live with the candle alight at both ends, with all scruples and principles thrown aside, and every desire indulged to the full. Because of its geographical position – Corinth was easily reached by sea, and was a most important port in the East–West Mediterranean traffic – it had a very mixed population with a large number of travellers, traders and hangers-on. It was probably not intrinsically any more wicked than any other sea-port, but its reputation for sexual licence had largely grown because it had been for hundreds of years a centre for the organised worship of the goddess of Love (first Aphrodite and now in Roman times, Venus). As always happens where there is such widespread sexual licence, there sprang up a host of vicious fellow-travellers – greed, blackmail, cheating, slander, perversion and the rest.

I had a fair picture of the sort of place it must have been, and indeed of what an unlikely place it must have seemed for the founding of a Christian church, when I suddenly came across 1 Corinthians 6: 11. Paul has just recounted some of the more repulsive sins to which human beings can sink and has assured his hearers that the Kingdom of God cannot be the possession of people like that, when suddenly he writes, AND SUCH WERE SOME OF YOU!

### EVIDENCE OF SOMETHING SUPER-HUMAN

I had never realised what an astonishing piece of Christian evidence this is. No one doubts that this is an authentic Letter of Paul, probably written some ten years before the first Gospel was set down. And here, to people living in this centre of idolatry and all kinds of human depravity Paul can write "and such were some of you"! What, I ask, and shall continue to ask of my non-Christian friends, is supposed to have changed these men and women so fundamentally? The personality of Paul? The most casual reading of his two surviving Letters to Corinth will quickly show that even among his converts he was not universally admired. It seems obvious that something very unusual had happened and was happening. People, sometimes the most unlikely people, were being converted in heart and mind by *something*. To Paul and his fellow apostles it was plainly the invasion of the human spirit by God's own Spirit. The power required to convert and to sustain the new life *naturally*, was to Paul another manifestation of the power which God showed in raising Jesus from the dead. The "fruits of the Spirit" which Paul lists in the fifth chapter of his Letter to the Galatians are not the result of fearful effort and tormenting self-denial. They are fruits: they grow naturally, once the living Spirit of God is allowed to enter a man's inner being.

Here then, are two miracles: the transformation of human nature from within and the raising of the man Jesus from death. According to Paul's Gospel they are both demonstrations of God's power in the midst of human circumstances and in spite of human probability.

I do not propose to linger long here on the well-known prose-poem about Christian love which is in the thirteenth chapter. I do not think that its authority is in question, and I will merely comment, for the benefit of those who sometimes find Paul irritating, that this must be the work of a man of rare insight and equally rare poetic genius. It is in itself a miracle that a man with the training of Saul of Tarsus should see with such clarity that without "love" every scrap of learning and achievement, every strenuous effort and every painful sacrifice amount to nothing at all.

Then I came to the fifteenth chapter, which I have come to regard in some ways as the most important chapter in the New Testament. Certainly it is the earliest evidence for the resurrection of Christ. We need to remind ourselves that so far there were no written Gospels, and that these words were written some twenty years after the crucifixion of Jesus. There would still be many alive who knew and remembered him, and Paul lists some of those who saw Christ alive after his very public death. I was struck again by the "over five hundred Christians" who saw Jesus simultaneously, "of whom", Paul comments, "the majority are still alive". The evidence for the resurrection does not rest on hysterical visions in the half-light of early dawn but on actual "appearances", the last of which seems to have happened to Paul. I noticed the flat, matter-of-fact recital of known events. There is no attempt to persuade or prove, and certainly there is no artistic embellishment. Paul is, in effect, saying: these are the historic facts which we know.

Then, at verse twelve, he does allow himself to be moved. Since the risen Christ convinced him, and since the risen Christ is the power behind the gospel he preaches, as well as the author of the faith which has grown up in the unlikely soil of Corinth, how *can* anyone, even for the sake of argument, deny that Christ really rose?

I confess that I was as much astonished as Paul that *Christians* should not believe in the life that is to follow this obviously incomplete and imperfect one. During the years of the war, when death could strike at anyone with little or no warning, it was not thought morbid but merely commonsense to consider what happens to us after our bodies "die". I had several hundred conversations with those who were bereaved, and I believe that these inspired words of long ago brought reassurance to many. We learned to accept our mortality, and our faith in Christ's promises was greatly strengthened.

But since the war ended it seems that quite a proportion of professing Christians do not really believe in any life after this temporal one. Recently I read that the 1964 Gallup Poll gave to ABC Television the following percentages: 88 per cent of regular Roman Catholics, 86 per cent of regular Non-Conformists, 85 per cent of regular Church of England attenders believe in life after death. Since faith in the resurrection of Christ and the sharing of his timeless life has always been an integral part of the Gospel, I cannot help wondering why quite a proportion of those who accept Christianity stop short of its most valuable promise.


## "ETERNITY" IS NOT EXTENDED TIME

It may be that there is some lack of imagination. If we speak loosely of "eternity", some people think that we mean millions of years plus millions of years *ad infinitum*. They do not seem able to grasp the fact that once we are outside the time-and-space set-up (in which we are in this life inescapably confined), neither "time" nor "space" has any meaning. There may be all kinds of "dimensions" of which we are at present ignorant, and for which there are no descriptive words.

But I believe Paul himself puts his finger on the nub of the matter in verse thirty-five on this same chapter.

Some people then, as some people now, seemed to envisage this temporary corruptible body being magically revived, and to think that this is what is meant by "resurrection". Of course it is not. Paul is at pains to explain that even on this planet the "body" which contains the life is adapted to the environment – fish, birds, animals are all different, while the "celestial bodies" to be observed in the sky are completely and splendidly unlike anything earthly.

God gives us the "spiritual" body suitable for the new environment for which we are destined as sons of God. We can be sure of that, and the resurrection of Christ is our guarantee. We can be equally sure that "the transitory could never possess the everlasting". (v. 50) Indeed who would wish for this old, weary, diseased, and possibly maimed body to be somehow newly injected with life? We know perfectly well that human flesh eventually decays, quickly by fire or slowly by decomposition in the earth, whatever the "morticians" of America would have us believe.

Why then does Paul insist on a "body" at all? It is because he is concerned to defend the Christian belief in man's resurrection after the pattern of Christ's resurrection. The old Greek belief, and its Roman counterpart, held that once the body was dead the disembodied soul lived in a miserable twilight existence in Hades. It was the place of shadows and shades, the dark and joyless limbo of the departed. The Hebrew idea of Sheol was very little different. Sadness, silence and hopelessness seemed to brood over the life after death. The men and women of Corinth would probably have heard of both Hades and Sheol. They might also have heard vaguely of the Greek philosophers' concept of the immortality of the human soul.

But death was to men of those days the ultimate disaster. It may be that some of these Corinthians could not accept the miserable twilight of such places as Hades or Sheol and that the persistence of the "soul" seemed no more than a philosopher's speculation. It may be that to believe in annihilation at death seemed to them the best way to meet it.

This negative thinking Paul is determined to correct. The resurrection of Christ was always to him the key to the human dilemma. Christ had become man, Christ had died for man, and Christ had risen to open the door to the glories that human vocabulary has no words to describe. Paul knew that man's last enemy, death, was now defeated, and men could look forward, not to a shadowy half-life, but to a life fuller and more glorious than human imagination can conceive. No more nonsense, he urges, about what sort of "body" we shall possess when these mortal bodies perish. That we can safely leave to God, who has demonstrated the defeat of death by the raising up of Christ.

## NEW TESTAMENT CERTAINTY

For me, the translator, this fifteenth chapter seemed alive and vibrant, not with pious hope, but with inspired certainty. Quite suddenly I realised that *no man had ever written such words before*. As I pressed on with the task of translation I came to feel utterly convinced of the truth of the resurrection. Something of literally life-and-death importance had happened in mortal history, and I was reading the actual words of people who had seen Christ after his resurrection and had seen men and women deeply changed by his living power. Previously, although I had known something of the "comfort of the Scriptures" and had never thought them to be false, I must have been insulated from their reality simply because they were known as "scripture". Now I was compelled to come to the closest possible terms with this writing and I was enormously impressed, and still am. On the one hand these Letters were written over quite a period of years, but there is not the slightest discernible diminution of faith. And on the other hand it was borne in upon me with irresistible force that these Letters could never have been written at all if there had been no Jesus Christ, no crucifixion and no resurrection.

The more I thought about it, the more unthinkable it became that any of this new courageous, joyful life could have originated in any kind of concocted story or wishful thinking. There had been a stupendous Event, and from that was flowing all this strength and utter conviction.

I was, and indeed am, impressed by the fact that the New Testament letters were written not in some holy retreat but sometimes from prison, sometimes from ordinary, probably Christian, homes. Moreover, they were written to people who were called to live Christian lives in a thoroughly pagan world. Moral standards of all kinds were low and there was nothing remotely resembling a Christian public opinion. There were no Sundays, no church buildings and very little leisure for most people. Slavery was, of course, everywhere, and so were dire poverty and unrelieved sickness and disease. The great persecutions had not yet started but the smaller ones had. A man could lose not only his friends but his livelihood in a place like Ephesus if it became known publicly that he did not believe in the goddess Diana. A man could easily be looked at askance if he disowned the local gods, and he could be considered very odd if he broke with his previous companions in alcoholic revellings. And it could have been very easy to frame a charge against a man who set Jesus Christ above the Emperor of the Roman Empire.

## THE VIGOUR OF THE FAITH

It was against such a background of mixed paganism that the Christian faith began to grow and expand. Even if I were not myself a convinced Christian I should find it impossible to explain this strange phenomenon. If we had records of a few emotional meetings, the effects of which were merely transient, we could write the whole Christian movement off as one of those passing waves of superstition which did from time to time disturb the pagan world. But we have no such thing: we have as good solid evidence of a strong and growing faith as any historian could require. Let us, for a moment, discount the Gospel stories as written-up histories of a hero long since dead. (I do not myself think of the four Gospels like this, as I hope to show.) Even without the evidence of the books attributed to the four evangelists, we have the strongest possible evidence for the early days of Christianity from the Letters of Paul, James, Peter and John. It is *letters* which are of unique value to the historian who is trying to record the actual events of any period. Newspapers, and before them broadsheets and pamphlets, naturally have their worth, but they are likely to be slanted one way or another. But if the historian can lay his hands upon a packet of letters he has priceless evidence for the period of which he is writing. For letters, speaking generally, are not written with any political axe to grind nor are they usually written for posterity. They reflect accurately the times in which they are written.

So it is with the New Testament Epistles. I doubt very much whether any of their writers had any idea that he was writing "Holy Scripture". For the most part of it was "*ad hoc*" writing: a particular situation, or even the behaviour of a particular person or group, called for the writing of the letter. Yet all of them, from their different points of view, bear witness to the growing of a new society of men and women quite different from the Greek, Roman Jewish or pagan pattern. The whole movement is based on the fact (about which no New Testament writer argues) that Jesus Christ was God and man. He is now "the Lord", and every system of thinking and every way of action must be decided not merely by reference to his example and teaching but by the leading of his active living Spirit.

## THE STRENGTH OF CONCERTED EVIDENCE

As I continued this close association with the New Testament Epistles (on one full morning each week, for there was plenty of other work to be done!), I found an extraordinary unanimity of spirit. I say "extraordinary" because superficially Paul, James, John and Peter are poles apart in temperament, and widely different in their presentation of the Christian Gospel. But this difference is only superficial: it soon becomes plain that they are all speaking of the same thing and, further, that their messages are complementary rather than contradictory. I have heard professing Christians of our own day speak as though the historicity of the Gospels does not matter – all that matters is the contemporary Spirit of Christ. I contend that the historicity does matter, and I do not see why we, who live nearly two thousand years later, should call into question an Event for which there were many eye-witnesses still living at the time when most of the New Testament was written. It was no "cunningly devised fable" but an historic irruption of God into human history which gave birth to a young Church so sturdy that the pagan world could not stifle or destroy it.

## SOME RE-DISCOVERIES

As this New Testament world became more and more real to me, I found several facets of the faith which were bright and shining then but which have become dulled and obscure in our modern discipleship. The first is what Paul calls the "mystery" which has been hidden through all the ages until that time. (Col. 1: 26). It is simply that Christ lives *in* the personality of the man who believes in him, and brings with him the hope of "glory" to come. No other religion dares to say such a thing about the person whom men worship as God. God had always been *external*, the power to be obeyed. Now at last the wonder which we should never have had the impertinence to claim, is seen to have come true in Christ. Not only has God become man and lived life on human terms; not only has God reconciled man to himself by a personal act; not only has God proved that death is conquered by an unforgettable demonstration of power, but God lives *in* the man whose personality is open to him. Life is a matter not of conforming to external rules but of being transformed from within.

## THE GOD WITHIN US

This truth, which is mentioned again and again in the New Testament, seems to us too good to be true. We labour and strive and pray as though Christianity were a difficult *performance*. Theoretically we would agree with the notion of the "indwelling Christ", but most of us for most of the time act as though we did not. We have lost sight of the fact that Christ is *in us*, both willing and doing. Consequently we lack that joy, confidence and spontaneity which rightly belongs to the sons of God. This does not, naturally, make our path smooth and free from trouble – neither Jesus nor Paul lived that kind of life. But it makes a whole world of difference when we believe that God, the whole unimaginable power, love and wisdom behind everything, is not merely on our side but actually at work in our hearts and minds.

Of course we believe this in part, and we in the Anglican Church make a special effort to believe it at such times as Confirmation, when the presence of the Holy Spirit is confirmed to the candidate by the laying on of the Bishop's hands. But, alas, how few appear to retain their faith in this super-human presence even for a few months! I blame no one, for I am also a priest and know how difficult it is to communicate a truth at once so simple and so profound.

But how far removed from the idea of the New Testament are the insipid words of the hymn which says "he came sweet influence to impart, a gracious willing guest", and goes on to say, "and his that gentle voice we hear soft as the breath of even, that checks each fault, that calms each fear . . ." Anyone who has any experience at all of the living God knows that he is nothing at all like this somebody who tut-tuts politely at our failings and lays a soothing hand upon our anxious little heads. The God who lives in us if we allow him, is not necessarily always gentle: he can be wind and fire and a whole lot of other things. He can give us strength, but he can also show us our weakness! He will "increase our faith", but frequently not in the way we want or expect. He will show us, as we can bear it, more and more truth, but he will shatter our illusions without scruple, perhaps especially illusions about ourselves. He will give us moments of wonderful perception, but will also allow us to endure terrifying darkness. His dealings with us are not some optional religious game; he is in deadly earnest and he is intent on "bringing many sons to glory". He is indeed all goodness and light but he will show no more compunction towards the evil things that we have allowed to grow in our hearts than a human surgeon would to a malignant growth. The men of old were hardly exaggerating when they said, "Our God is a consuming fire".

## THE IMAGINED GOD — AND THE REAL

I suspect that in our pride we would prefer to have an external God, i.e. one who makes unreasonable demands on us and fails to keep what seems to be the one elementary rule for God – that if we lead good lives we shall (by right) be protected from all the painful and nasty things that happen to other people. It is an easy step from this to atheism. God having plainly failed and we having plainly outgrown him, then we must fall back on ourselves.

Yes, we must, but we do not thereby escape our dealings with God, for it is here in ourselves, that he will, given half a chance, come to live and start putting our house in order! A little bit of us wants this, and a big babyish part of us does not: it refuses to grow up. We would rather be men with a grievance against an imaginary God than have any truck with the real, living God, who, if once we allowed him in, might get up to all sorts of things.

Yes, indeed he might, but we are both wrong and foolish to be afraid. For one thing we cannot in the long run win any battle against the unceasing pressure of God's love, and for another he who appears to be our enemy is not merely our friend but someone who is in closest harmony with our deepest self. "We are not," said Von Hügel, "to think of the Holy Spirit and the human spirit, God and the soul, as two separate entities. God's Spirit works in closest associations with ours."* And in any case, although God may hurt us, he will never harm us, since his nature is Love of the highest kind.

## "THE LIVING GOD" POTENT AND CONTEMPORARY

It seemed, and seems, to me that in the New Testament we have men and women whose lives have been invaded by the living Spirit of God. They are not thereby made instantaneously perfect, as we can see and as they would be the first to admit. But they *are* being transformed and they *are* aware of their new relationship with God and with one another. I cannot believe that this wonderful new factor in human living – and I must underline its newness – was meant to taper off and disappear as the years passed. It is surely part of the everlasting Gospel that God lives and works *in* a man, whether he lives in the first or the twentieth century. It is part of our incredible modern blindness that we fail to see this as the best of good news! And such is the prevailing de-Godded atmosphere that most men see no need for the Gospel at all, and even Christians to some degree miss the wonder of the divine invasion.

I think this sense of the reality of God, both in himself, so to speak, and at work so plainly in human beings is perhaps the great fascination of the New Testament. It

* Quoted by H. A. Williams on p. 18 of *The True Wilderness.*

may make us wistful; we may long to warm our hands at the fires that are blazing there. It may make us determined to break the tyranny of modern thought-forms which have set such disastrous limits upon our powers of belief. But at least, if we are as honest and as unprejudiced as possible, we are obliged to admit that here is authentic, unpretentious writing, describing in almost everyday terms what to us is a most unlikely miracle – the transformation of human character by the entrance of the love of God. Here is the first and most deadly casualty in our modern pattern of thought: that we do not seriously believe that God is willing to penetrate the inner springs of human character and begin a salutary revolution there. This disbelief is our incalculable loss.


THE PRESENT REALITY OF EVIL

The second difference between New Testament thinking and that of our day is that the powers of evil, whether outside or inside the human personality, are never nowadays taken to have any real existence. We willingly admit to being maladjusted or repressed or deprived, and we are quite willing to have psychiatry explain our delinquencies and sins, but we do not usually admit the existence of "evil". Now to men like Paul, John, Peter and James right and wrong existed as surely as light and darkness. The Christian's way was a tough and difficult battle and to win it he needed "the whole armour of God". Theirs was a spiritual struggle against the unseen forces of evil.

If we talk or preach today about the reality of evil we are accused of "Dualism", which is a technical term meaning that this world has really two gods, the God who is all that is good, and Satan who is all that is evil. If one's critics mean that we believe in the permanent existence of

Satan, the Devil or the powers of evil, they are wrong, for we do not. Once we have passed from this stage of existence into the one Christ has prepared for us "Satan" ceases to exist. But for the time being the power of evil to obstruct, confuse, corrupt, seduce, dissuade – all the unholy battery by which the Christian is assailed – is real, and is to be fought and defeated.

If someone cannot grasp how a fact of this life can cease to be a fact in some other mode of existence, we need look no further for an illustration than our own bodies. For the time being they are real enough, and we must feed and clothe and wash and generally look after them, No one but a madman believes that his body has no reality, and even the strictest ascetic has to eat and drink unless he is bent on suicide. These bodies are real, but only temporarily so. As we have already seen, they are doomed to physical dissolution sooner or later. In another world they cease to be. So it is with the powers of evil. They are "temporary" in the sense that they are limited to this life, but to regard them as anything less than real in the here-and-now can be most dangerous.

All this is nonsense to the uncommitted agnostic, but it is sober truth to the man who is honestly committed to the way of Christ. I have never yet met a Christian who was not tempted, sometimes severely and for a long time, and I don't think I have ever met an agnostic who has any idea of what we mean by our battle against spiritual powers of evil. The New Testament view makes better sense to me than the best of humanism, as well as describing something far more like my own experience and that of the Christians I know. There *is* a struggle, sometimes a very bitter and difficult one, and it is not merely against "absence of good" or "ignorance" or "the amoral unconscious mind". Maybe it is against these, but the sense of conflict against actual evil which the Christian has

35

to fight is as real in his experience as any other part of his observed existence.

Jesus apparently spoke of "Satan", "the Devil", "the prince of this world" and "the wicked one". Paul wrote of "Satan", "the god of this world", "the devil" and in the famous sixth chapter of his Letter to the Ephesians he speaks of the battle of the Christian "against principalities, against powers, against the rulers of the darkness of this world, against spiritual wickedness in high places". Peter warned his readers that their "adversary the devil, as a roaring lion, walketh about, seeking whom he may devour". James gave the advice to "resist the devil, and he will flee from you". John refers several times to "the devil", the "children of the devil" and "the works of the devil", and, in speaking of the Christian's battle, he reminds his readers that "greater is he that is in you than he that is in the world".

There is no need at all for us to revert to medieval crudity and to conjure up a whole picture-gallery of devils. But it is quite as unrealistic to suppose that there is no adversary, no sower of doubts and fears, no tempter to corrupt our best endeavours. Jesus used the name Satan for this evil force, presumably because it was current in his day and his hearers would know what he was talking about. But, just as he never argued about the existence of God, so he accepted as a fact of life this evil power which can, at any time, destroy or corrupt. It is noteworthy that when Peter was once inspired to see who Jesus really was, Jesus congratulated him on the insight given to him, and almost at once rebuked him sternly as "Satan", for suggesting a course that would be contrary to the plan of God. (Matt. 16: 23) I quote here from a recent book: "Anyone who has ever tried to formulate a private prayer in silence, and in his own heart, will know what I mean by *diabolical interference*. The forces of evil are in opposition to the will of God. And the nearer a man's will approaches God's, the more apparent and stronger and more formidable this opposition is seen to be. It is only when we are going in more or less the same direction as the devil that we are unconscious of any opposition at all."* These sentences are completely true to my own experience of life and to that of my Christian friends and correspondents. The battle of which the New Testament speaks so realistically is still raging, and every Christian finds himself involved in it. This is one more reason why these ancient writings ring so true in modern ears.


## THIS WORLD AND THE NEXT

The third element which sounds strongly throughout the New Testament is the conviction that earthly life is no more than a temporary pilgrimage. Heaven, even though there are no earthly words to describe it, is ever-present in the minds of the inspired writers. The words of Paul, which I have already quoted, succinctly describe their common conviction: "I reckon that the sufferings of this present time are not worthy to be compared with the glory which shall be revealed in us."

To many moderns this sounds almost unbearably naïve —as does any idea of reward or punishment in a future life. We must do good, we are told, for the sake of doing good. Similarly we must not hurt others because it is a bad thing to do so. In either case we must put out of

* *Of Heaven and Hope* by David Bolt (Hodder and Stoughton).

our minds any idea of a life to come – that is pure wishful-thinking and belongs to the romantic infancy of religion.

I believe that by cutting out the whole realm of spiritual reality (of which this little life is a mere outcrop in time and space) we are robbing ourselves of more than we know. Instead of being sons of God with unlimited potentialities when our present probation is over, we are merely decent humanists with a possible tinge of Christian piety. We have lost a whole dimension, a dimension which the New Testament either robustly asserts or tacitly assumes to be the true and lasting one. We thereby automatically make most of its truth either meaningless or at best a mythical parable.

## PAUL KNEW MORE THAN WE THINK

I believe that the best cure for this peculiar state of mind is to study, (or re-study) the Letters and actions of a man like Paul. I myself found as I studied his writings that his mind was far more acute than I had thought, and his imagination quite extraordinary in a man of such immense moral and physical courage. I would further say that we moderns tend to underestimate the intelligence of people like Paul. Because such a man had never seen a bicycle, a typewriter or a television set we, perhaps unconsciously, look down on him as living in some sort of twilight ignorance. We forget that he lived in point of time very close to the historic events described in the New Testament, and that he had plenty of opportunity to check their authenticity from many eye-witnesses. We forget, too, that he knew the philosophies of Greece not merely as text-book subjects but as systems of thought being taught and practised in his day. When he wrote to the Colossians and warned them of "philosophy and vain deceit", he was not being anti-intellectual. He knew from observation as well as from personal knowledge of human beings that philosophy, however attractive intellectually, is sterile and impotent when it comes to changing human disposition.

### GOD IS NOT A MAGNIFIED MAN!

The fourth remarkable feature of New Testament thinking is the combining of a sense of the immensity of God's wisdom and power with a sure knowledge of his infinite love for each individual person. Thus what seems to be a particular difficulty to the modern thinker is not so regarded by Paul and the others. It does not seem to them incongruous that the wisdom and love of God should operate on a vast scale towards whole nations or worlds, and at the same time care intimately for each separate human being. We exaggerate the difficulty, for if we are not careful we persist in regarding God as a man magnified to the $n$th degree. We know very well that in matters of human government, however liberal or benevolent, a man is no more than a unit. The elected power is concerned with the well-being of the community as a whole, and cannot possibly be concerned in any intimate way with any individual life. Unless, therefore, we think seriously of what we mean by "God" we constantly transfer this kind of attitude to our creator. Further, now that we know so much more about the structure of the observable universe, whether in terms of size, speed, power or complexity, men too easily assume that one isolated person cannot possibly matter to the vast mind behind it. Even worse, because a thing is beyond man's imagination he dismisses it as impossible. But the New Testament, as, to be fair, does the Old, insists that God is not man.

What is impossible to men is perfectly possible to God. I am not a theologian, and neither, I imagine, are most of my readers, and words are slippery things to use when we are talking about God. But surely the chief glory of the Christian Gospel is to declare the unremitting purpose of God's love towards his whole creation; to declare that God became man both to show how life should be lived and to make reconciliation between the evils that are in man and the perfection which belongs to God; and to overcome man's last and darkest enemy, death. The Gospel also declares that the invisible Spirit of God works in and through human beings whenever and wherever he is allowed to transform and guide.

### GOD'S "COMPREHENSIVE" LOVE

We may find it difficult to hold all these thoughts in our minds simultaneously, but they fairly represent the way in which the New Testament writers looked at God, man and life. Paul, for example, with his Jewish upbringing and pharisaic training would have a highly exalted view of the one true God, but after his conversion he also knows that the same God whose wisdom is unsearchable is his Father and he can speak personally and naturally of Jesus Christ as "the Son of God who loved me and gave himself for me". In my experience of people I have found that among committed Christians this "comprehensive" view of God as both the creator of infinite wisdom and power and as the Father caring deeply for the individual is a quite ordinary phenomenon. It is the agnostic or the would-be atheist who produces and magnifies the intellectual difficulty. No one in his senses would pretend that God is anything but a vast unfathomable mystery, and nothing is more repugnant as well as impertinent than that attitude of over-familiarity which suggests that we are now old enough to talk on equal terms with the creator. Nevertheless it remains true that a human being can in a real sense "know" God through Christ, and Christ himself can be truly alive to him. I have seen this recognition and knowledge of God in people of all denominations, in men and women of several different nationalities as well as in those who belong to various social strata. I have known extremely clever scientists as well as men of the highest calibre in literature or the arts who regard God with the deepest awe and at the same time know him through Christ almost as a personal friend. I have also known people of a much simpler cast of mind, who would probably not be able to pass any formal examination, who have a sturdy and invincible faith in God their Father and similarly find Christ a real person. It is true that the comparatively unintelligent will sometimes use naïve terms in speaking of God, but I have never found a true Christian without a profound sense of awe and wonder. I cannot help being impressed by what I have seen and by what people have told me. The laboratory-check for spiritual experience is life itself, and it is exactly here, sometimes in the most appallingly dangerous and painful situations that I have found faith both sure and radiant. In short, I have seen the experience of God described in the New Testament occurring again and again in our modern world.

## THE FOLLY OF TAKING SIMILES LITERALLY

There is an idea current among some New Testament scholars that people like Paul had a primitive system of thought – that theirs was a three-decker universe, with "heaven" above, "hell" below, and "earth" in between.

For myself I seriously doubt this. In the intensive reading which translation requires I formed the strong impression that so far from trying to fit ideas of God into any preconceived concept, Paul is struggling with human words to express something of the wonders which, he senses, lie beyond observable life. To him it is the things which are seen which are temporal; it is the unseen things which are eternal. I find it hard to be patient with modern critics who assume that when Paul speaks of Christ's ascending "up on high" or when he urges the Colossians to "seek those things which are above, where Christ sitteth at the right hand of God", he is really talking of some location a certain number of miles above the earth's surface. There is a disquieting confusion of thought here. I think I can understand the Russian astronaut who is reputed to have said on his return from orbit that now he knew that there was no God since he had been out in space and there was no one there. This shows merely a peasant's-eye view of religion. But there are several modern writers who pour scorn upon any idea of God being *up* or *above*. They are confusing literal spatial position with a mental image which must be common to nearly all thinking human beings. Why should we talk of "high" ideals or a "high" purpose? Why should we talk of a "rise" in salary? Why should sales be "soaring"? Why should a boy be promoted from the *Lower* to the *Upper* Vth form? Why does an important person in our judiciary sit in a *high* court? And so we could go on. It is a common and quite understandably symbolic way of speaking, and naturally the converse of it is equally true. For example in ordinary speech a man may *fall* in our estimation, a failing business is fast going *downhill*, some people are of *low* intelligence and some unfortunates have sunk to the *depths*, etc.

As I studied Paul's Letters I became convinced that he

uses expressions of height and depth as useful symbols but not as geographical locations. When, for example, he writes that "God raised Christ from the dead and set him at his own right hand in the heavenly places, far above all principality and power, and might, and dominion, and every name that is named, not only in this world, but also in that which is to come", does anyone seriously imagine that Paul, or the Ephesian Christians to whom he was writing, thought of this exaltation as being measurable in physical terms? Again, in the same Letter to Ephesus, when Paul asserts that the Christian's real battle is against spiritual rather than physical enemies and mentions "spiritual wickedness in high places", does anyone seriously suggest that Paul meant demonic goings-on at the Emperor's court? Of course not! To Paul there was the heavenly reality which at present we may sense but not see, and the earthly reality which is discernible by the senses but doomed, like all creation, to ultimate decay. The "bright blue sky" stuff belongs to Victorian piety and not to the New Testament.

### THE NECESSITY FOR PICTURE-LANGUAGE

I feel I must record here my sense of injustice that the Christian religion should be singled out as a target for criticism because it uses, and is bound to use, "picture-language". We all do it every day of our lives, and we are none the worse for it. No one blames the accountant for talking of a "balance", the economist for speaking of "frozen assets", the electronics engineer for talking of a magnetic "field", the traffic controller for referring to a "peak" period, the electrical engineer for speaking of "load-shedding" or the town-planner for talking of a "bottle-neck". Not one of these words is literally true but

43

they convey quickly, and pretty accurately, an idea which can be readily understood. I cannot see why we, who accept hundreds of such usages in everyday speaking and writing, should decide that an expression such as "seated at the right hand of the Father" is either literally true or totally false.

But just as there is a real situation behind each of the shorthand "pictures" which I have given above so there is a reality behind every Christian expression. Because picture-language is sometimes used it does not follow that the actual events are unhistorical or "mythical". The strange thing to me is that so few New Testament expressions need explanation. There are obvious exceptions: the Epistle to the Hebrews was especially written for the Hebrew mind and necessarily contains many ideas and expressions which are strange to the non-Jew. But on the whole the technical expressions are few and the "pictures" easily understood. Given a good translation, there is little in the New Testament letters which the modern reader will find dated or irrelevant. Indeed, as I said in a slightly different context above, I have literally hundreds of letters written from all parts of the English-speaking world which prove this very point. And although the difficulties are very much greater, those who have, with enormous care and sympathy, translated the epistles into many other languages have found a similar response. The British and the American Bible Societies have an impressive record of the relevance of the New Testament epistles to life as people of very different backgrounds and cultures have to live it today.

Just over two hundred years ago, in 1754 to be precise, Horace Walpole coined the word "serendipity" which has now come to be accepted into our language. The word, which is derived from the ancient name for Ceylon, is defined as "the faculty of making happy and unexpected discoveries by accident". Before I go on to discuss the work of translating the Gospels I feel I must mention some of the "happy and unexpected discoveries" which I made in the translation of the Epistles.

### SERENDIPITY: 1

The first one I will mention, which of course may all the time have been no secret to anybody else, was the expression "rich in mercy". (Eph. 2: 4) This struck me as a positive jewel. Just as we might say that a Texas tycoon is "rich in oil", so Paul writes it as a matter of fact that God is "rich in mercy". The pagan world was full of fear, and the Christian Gospel set out to replace that fear of the gods or the fates, or even life itself, with love for and trust in God. "Rich in mercy" was Good News to the ancient world and it is Good News today.

### SERENDIPITY: 2

I think the idea of God's personal care for the individual came upon me with a similar unexpected strength when I came to translate 1 Peter 5: 7, which reads in the Authorised Version "casting all your care upon him; for he careth for you". In one sense it is quite plain that God wants us to bear responsibility; it is a false religion which teaches that God wants us to be permanently immature. But there is a sense in which the conscientious and the imaginative can be overburdened. This familiar text reminded me that such over-anxiety can be "off-loaded" on to God for each one of us is his personal concern. The "text" is commonplace enough, perhaps too commonplace, for it was not until I had to translate it that I came to realise something of its full force. The word used for "casting" is an almost violent word, conveying the way in which a man at the end of his tether might throw aside an intolerable burden. And the Christian is recommended to throw this humanly insupportable weight upon the only one who can bear it and at the same time to realise that God cares for him intimately as a person. "He careth for you" is hardly strong enough and I don't know that I did much better in rendering the words "you are his personal concern". The Greek words certainly mean this but probably more. It is not the least glory of the Christian Gospel that the God revealed by Jesus Christ possesses wisdom and power beyond all human imagining but never loses sight of any individual human being. It may seem strange to us and it may seem an idea quite beyond our little minds to comprehend, but each one of us *matters* to God. It is of course the same sense of intimate concern which Jesus expressed poetically when he assured us that even the hairs on our head are numbered. It is the kind of inspired truth of which we have continually to remind ourselves, if only because life so often apparently contradicts it.


SERENDIPITY: 3

I had for some time been worried about the expression "fear and trembling". It did not seem likely to me that

46

Paul in writing to the Philippians could have meant literally that they were to work out their salvation in a condition of anxiety and nervousness. We all know that fear destroys love and spoils relationships, and a great deal of the New Testament is taken up with getting rid of the old ideas of fear and substituting the new ideas of love and trust. I realised that the Greek word translated "fear" can equally well mean "reverence" or "awe" or even "respect", but I was bothered about the "trembling". Surely the same Spirit who inspired Paul to write to Timothy that "God hath not given us the spirit of fear; but of power and of love and of a sound mind" could not also have meant us to live our entire lives in a state of nervous terror. I came to the conclusion, a little reluctantly, that the expression "in fear and trembling" had become a bit of a cliché, even as it has in some circles today. As I went on translating I found that this must be the case. For when Paul wrote to the Corinthians and reported that Titus had been encouraged and refreshed by their reception of him, he then goes on to say that the Corinthian Christians received him with "fear and trembling"! (2 Cor. 7: 15) Now this makes nonsense, unless it is a purely conventional verbal form implying proper respect. For, little as we know of Titus, we cannot imagine any real Christian minister being encouraged and refreshed by a display of nervous anxiety. We get the same phrase occurring again in Paul's advice to Christian slaves (Eph. 6: 5), where the context makes it quite clear that faithfulness and responsibility are much more what Paul means than "fear and trembling". This much became plain, and then I realised that when Paul really did mean the words to be taken literally he amplified them to make sure they would be properly understood. I think we sometimes imagine that the incredibly heroic Paul suffered from no human weaknesses, except for the "thorn in the flesh" about which all New Testament commentators have written. (2 Cor. 12: 7) But if we turn to 1 Cor. 2: 3 we find Paul writing that "I was with you in weakness, and in fear, and in much trembling". Now this is a different thing altogether. Here we have a man honest enough to admit that he was frightened and that he was, or had been, ill. "Fear and trembling" here are perfectly legitimate. It is only when they are used as a phrase almost without literal meaning that we begin to feel uncomfortable.

### SERENDIPITY: 4

This leads me on to another heartening discovery, which I made in 2 Cor. 1: 8ff. I had not previously realised that even a man of such indomitable courage as Paul, filled as he undoubtedly was with the Spirit of the living God, could nevertheless be "pressed out of measure, above strength, insomuch that we despaired even of life". We lesser mortals, who live infinitely less adventurous lives, may sometimes experience something of this pressure. It is not that we, any more than Paul, despair of God as far as the ultimate outcome is concerned. But we can be over-come by the most terrifying darkness and reduced to a sense of inadequacy amounting to near desperation. Again, it was not until I came to the close study of this passage that I realised under what fearful pressure Paul must at times have been. I further came to see that the "stiff upper lip" business is not necessarily Christian; it sounds much more like a throw-back to the Stoics than to early Christianity. For although the New Testament abounds in advice to men to be strong and to master their fears it does not consider it disgraceful, for example, that a man might be moved even to tears, not indeed for himself but because he cared deeply for others. The letters tell no story of idealised human beings but reflect the life of people who are changed but by no means yet perfect.

## SERENDIPITY: 5

At some stage in my life as a Christian I must have heard the total depravity of man heavily emphasised. I do not think I ever personally accepted this, because ordinary observation showed a good deal of kindness and generosity produced by people whether they had religious faith or not. But I have found among gatherings of Christians of various denominations a minority who seemed to get a perverse delight in this emphasis on man's utter hopelessness. And indeed we have not got to look far into devotional literature, whether Protestant or Catholic, to come across the idea that man is hopelessly sinful and incapable of good without the operation of the grace of God. I am not at all proud of Article 13 in the Book of Common Prayer which says the same thing in a peculiarly unpleasant way. Now, to my joy, I found two delightful instances which could be quoted against the detractors of humanity if, as they sometimes do, they want to indulge in a text-slanging match! One comes from the first Epistle of John where the writer reminds his hearers that no one should deceive them by any clever talk, "The man who lives a consistently good life is a good man as surely as God is good". This truth is no more and no less than the saying of Christ himself when he said, "you will recognise them by their fruit; a good tree cannot produce bad fruit, any more than a bad tree can produce good fruit." This was a pleasant refreshment, but there was another wholly unexpected one at the end of the first

Epistle to the Corinthians (16: 13), where Paul urges his converts in the words "Quit you like men". (May I say in passing that these words from the Authorised Version are totally meaningless to the vast majority of young people.) But the literal translation is of course, "Be *men*". Now if it is true that man is so steeped in iniquity and incapable of goodness as some, especially in past centuries, would have us believe, there is no sense whatever in Paul's advice. But if it is true that the image of God is still present in man, however much it has been distorted or disfigured by evil, then it makes the most encouraging sense to be told to live like a man. At any rate I must put it on record that this is the effect the inspired words had upon me.

### SERENDIPITY: 6

A similar pleasant "discovery" came in 1 John 4: 7 in the words, "everyone that loveth is born of God, and knoweth God". Again, this inspired truth had naturally been there all the time, but I don't think I had ever heard a sermon preached on it. Throughout my years of experience it had struck me that the things that were really admirable in human behaviour were those inspired by love. I had also noticed, like many others, that people could exhibit most remarkable compassionate love without any great religious profession, or indeed with none at all. But if it is true, as John declares, that "God is love" it would make sense that any action that sprang from love had its origin in God. It would also mean that those who did give themselves in love to others did in fact "know God", however loudly they might protest their agnosticism. I have never been happy with any ecclesiastical or theological system in which correctness of belief was of paramount importance. It is only too easy for some men to build up a cerain theological structure which includes them and excludes others. But what we really believe in our heart of hearts may be quite different from what we outwardly profess. I saw then, and I have seen nothing in life to disturb this view, that when a man acts in response to love and compassion he is responding to God *whatever he thinks or says*. Conversely the man who refuses to become involved in the troubles and burdens of his fellows is rejecting God, however religious his outward profession may be.

SERENDIPITY: 7

"Beloved", wrote John, "now are we the sons of God, and it doth not yet appear what we shall be: but we know that, when he shall appear, we shall be like him; for we shall see him as he is." (1 John 3: 2) These words, familiar as I think they must have been to me for years, were yet another shock for me as I came to translate them. For what would normally be sheer effrontery or even blasphemy is here written with cool confidence and authority. No one to my knowledge has ever written like these New Testament writers. Yet I was constantly aware that I was dealing not with exhortations or homilies but with letters written to people living in the midst of this world's business, people who were tempted and tried as we are, blinkered and frustrated and limited just as we are, yet with the same unquenchable flame of hope in their hearts as Christians have today. The material in this single verse is quite extraordinarily compressed; there is enough here for half a dozen useful sermons! But it is the *authority* which stabs the spirit broad awake. Paul and John wrote because they *knew*. The Christian revelation was not to them a tentative hypothesis, but the truth about God and men. They had known it by experience, and seen it demonstrated as a powerful force in the lives of men. The whole Christian pattern had to be lived against pagan darkness and frequently overt hostility. It required superhuman qualities to survive. Of course there were casualties – Demas was not the first nor the last deserter – but the amazing thing to me is that the Christian Gospel took root and flourished in many different, and indeed unlikely, places.

SERENDIPITY: 8

There was another unexpected treasure waiting for me in the Letter of James. I suppose we all look upon the many disappointments and pains of this life as somehow hostile to us. We either fight or we grimly endure. It was therefore a salutary surprise to me to discover that James recommends his Christian brothers to *welcome* the assorted trials and troubles to which we are all exposed. "Count it all joy" he writes "when you fall into divers [= all kinds of] temptations." (1 : 2) Frankly I had never even thought of thus turning our apparent losses into real gains! But I am convinced that it is the right attitude to adopt. This is no question of "being a martyr", as we said when we were children, but of accepting suffering and loss as an integral part of life. I think we moderns are influenced more than we know by current modes of thinking which assume that we have a "right" to be happy, a "right" to live without pain and somehow a "right" to be shielded from the ills which flesh is heir to. Evidently the early Christians thought no such thing. They quite plainly took it as an honour to suffer for Christ's sake, and here the advice is to accept all kinds of troubles, whether they are apparently for Christ's sake or not, as friends instead of resenting them as intruders. Now I know that this kind of teaching can easily degenerate into an unhealthy and perverse wallowing in trouble. But this is not, I think, the early Christian intention. It is just as much a Christian duty to rejoice with those who rejoice as it is to weep with those who weep; it is as important to enjoy what God has richly given to us as it is to accept good humouredly and patiently the troubles, set-backs, disappointments and griefs which are also part of the human pattern.

There are naturally many more happy and unexpected discoveries which I made over the years, some of them perhaps merely revealing how superficial must have been my previous knowledge of the New Testament Letters. But since this is a personal testimony, I have felt it right to mention some of the things which came to me with fresh and startling clarity. I have kept the best until last. It occurs in 1 John 3: 20. Like many others, I find myself something of a perfectionist, and if we don't watch ourselves this obsession for the perfect can make us arrogantly critical of other people, and in certain moods, desperately critical of ourselves. In this state of mind it is not really that I cannot subscribe to the doctrine of the Forgiveness of Sins, but that the tyrannical super-Me condemns and has no mercy on myself. Now, John, in his wisdom, points out in these inspired words, "if our heart condemn us, God is greater than our heart, and knoweth all things". This is a gentle but salutary rebuke to our assumption that we know better than God! God, on any showing is infinitely greater in wisdom and love than we are, and, unlike us, knows all the factors involved in human behaviour. We are guilty of certain things and these we must confess with all honesty and make reparation where possible. But there may be many factors in our lives for which we are not really to blame at all. We did not choose our heredity; we did not choose the bad, indifferent or excellent way in which we were brought up. This is naturally not to say that every wrong thing we do, or every fear or rage to which we are subject today, is due entirely to heredity, environment and upbringing. But it certainly does mean that we are in no position to judge ourselves; we simply must leave that to God who is our Father and "is greater than our heart and knoweth all things". It is almost as if John is saying, "if God loves us, who are we to be so high and mighty as to refuse to love ourselves?"

### THE TRANSLATING OF THE GOSPELS

I have so far been writing chiefly of my translation of the Epistles. I hesitated long before I entered the world of the Gospels. In retrospect I think this was largely due to natural caution. I could apparently, by dint of hard thinking and sympathy with both New Testament Greek and the twentieth-century reader, convey something of the electric energy of the Letters. I was not aiming so much at absolute accuracy as to try to produce in modern minds what I imagined the original Greek words produced in the minds of first century readers and hearers. But while I felt at liberty to disentangle some of Paul's complex arguments, or to paraphrase where direct translation would not make sense, I was not at all sure that I could find the same success in rendering the four Gospels into modern English. The problem was in many ways more difficult. For the most part the Gospels are straightforward narrative, and although there are obscurities and archaisms the general effect of the Authorised Version is one of simple beauty. I could not, and did not try to, rival that wonderful translation of 1611. I simply "forgot" as completely as I could familiar words and turns of phrase and translated the first century Greek into what I thought would be its modern equivalent in English.

I have already referred to my rather snobbish approach to New Testament Greek which had seemed to me poor in vocabulary, loose in construction and generally of small literary value. I have since revised that opinion considerably, but at the time of translation the overwhelming feeling was one of their true inspiration. I did not find myself worried by a rather uncertain chronology, or even by apparent discrepancies between the various accounts. But I was intensely conscious of the enormous importance of what was being described in these seemingly artless pages.

AN INTERVIEW WITH A FELLOW-TRANSLATOR

Some years before the publication of the New English Bible I was invited by the B.B.C. to discuss the problems of translation with Dr. E. V. Rieu, who had himself recently produced a translation of the four Gospels for Penguin Classics. Towards the end of the discussion Dr. Rieu was asked about his general approach to the task, and his reply was this:

"My personal reason for doing this was my own intense desire to satisfy myself as to the authenticity and the spiritual content of the Gospels. And, if I received any new light by an intensive study of the Greek originals, to pass it on to others. I approached them in the same spirit as I would have approached them had they been presented to me as recently discovered Greek manuscripts ..." A few minutes later I asked him, "Did you get the feeling that the whole material is extraordinarily alive? ... I got the feeling that the whole thing was alive even while one was translating. Even though one did a dozen versions of a particular passage, it was still living. Did you get that feeling?" Dr. Rieu replied :"I got the deepest feeling that I possibly could have expected. It ... changed me; my work changed me. And I came to the conclusion that these words bear the seal of ... the Son of Man and God. And they're the Magna Carta of the human spirit."

I found it particularly thrilling to hear a man who is a scholar of the first rank as well as a man of wisdom and experience openly admitting that these words written long ago were alive with power. They bore to him, as to me, the ring of truth.

## WHAT ARE THE "GOSPELS"?

The Gospels are not, in the modern sense, biographies. We have no idea of the physical stature or build of their chief subject, and no clue to his colouring. We do not know whether he had a powerful voice, although we may fairly infer that he was physically strong. Apart from one isolated incident, we have no information about his childhood, adolescence or young manhood and no record of the influences which formed his character. If we are looking for biography in the modern sense, we are disappointed. Some, like the late Albert Schweitzer, came to the conclusion that we never could know Jesus as a historical figure. And quite a number of scholars today would hold much the same view. The most we can do is to understand the meaning behind the "myths" of the Hellenic-Semitic world of first century Palestine. I cannot, as a translator, agree with this at all, except in one minor way, which I will return to later.

Suppose you are, as I was, translating with the mind emptied as far as possible of preconception. You cannot help noticing the differences between the hurried, almost breathless, style of Mark where almost everything seems to happen "straightway" and the much more elaborate Gospel of Matthew, who has a very definite purpose in view – to convince the Jews that Jesus was indeed the Messiah of whom the Old Testament prophets had spoken. Quite different again is the work of Luke, who appears to have made diligent research and unearthed some stories of Jesus which none of the other evangelists mention. Here, uniquely, are set down the concern of Jesus for women, for foreigners and for the underprivileged. To me it had all the marks of careful writing. And then came the problematical Fourth Gospel, which is a work of quite different character.

### A COMPOSITE PORTRAIT

Suppose that you have spent many hundred hours in putting these four widely differing accounts of some of the sayings and doings of the man Jesus into today's English. Do you find yourself so confused that you conclude that there was no such person at all? I take leave to doubt it. It is, in my experience, the people who have never troubled seriously to study the four Gospels who are loudest in their protests that there was no such person. I felt, and feel, without any shadow of doubt that close contact with the text of the Gospels builds up in the heart and mind a character of awe-inspiring stature and quality. I have read, in Greek and Latin, scores of myths but I did not find the slightest flavour of myth here. There is no hysteria, no careful working for effect and no attempt at collusion. These are not embroidered tales: the material is cut to the bone. One sensed again and again that understatement which we have been taught to think is more "British" than Oriental. There is an almost childlike candour and simplicity, and the total effect is tremendous. No man could ever have invented such a character as Jesus. No man could have set down such artless and vulnerable accounts as these unless some real Event lay behind them.

Thus the only small point which I will concede to the de-mythologisers is that several times I got the impression that the first three evangelists, naturally enough, did not quite realise what a world-shaking happening they were describing. But how could they? Their view of the world was small; their knowledge of history was limited. They did not know even what Paul knew of contemporary life around them. It is easy for us to feel that these men were ignorant peasants compared with ourselves who have advanced in knowledge over nearly two thousand years. If we do, we underestimate their intelligence and overestimate our own. Obviously they could not have anything approaching our historical perspective, but against this we must set the fact that they were living very much nearer to the actual point of time when Jesus was alive. There seems singularly little point in their concocting mythical stories about someone who never lived when violent persecution against those who followed the way of Jesus was well under way.

When I say that the first three Gospels at any rate are not biographies in the modern sense at all, I do not mean to say for one moment that I regard them as untrue. On the contrary, I believe them to be the verbal distillation of some of the things which Jesus said and did which the early evangelists felt constrained to put down in writing. It is impossible at this stage to say what their original sources were, and do not let us forget that in no case have we an original manuscript or anything like it. But from the major manuscripts and from the thousands of minor ones the textual experts are able to reconstruct with fair certainly what the evangelists wrote in the first instance. One thing is perfectly clear: these men were not in a conspiracy together or they would have been careful to avoid minor contradictions and discrepancies. The scholars who work out with enormous pains, through the evidence of style and vocabulary as well as from the content, the sources from which the evangelists worked are called form-critics. Of course, the whole business of form-criticism is as absorbing and exciting as the best of detective stories, and I think it would surprise the average layman to know, for example, to what lengths the form-critics will go in order to "prove" that some part of Luke's gospel belonged to another period of time, or indeed to another author than the rest of it.

## TITLES ARE NOT DIVINELY INSPIRED

I should not like it to be thought that I want to belittle the work of the form-critics, even though I sometimes cannot resist a smile at the way their views have changed over the last thirty years. But to me, as a translator, their work was largely irrelevant. I was dealing with material which was startlingly alive, and I could not really be overmuch bothered whether Matthew "borrowed" part of his Gospel story from Mark, or whether he and Mark shared a common source of written or spoken information which the critics call "Q". I know it is a shock to us today, and perhaps especially if we are professional writers and conscious of the laws of copyright, but it was not in the least strange in the first century A.D. to say that a gospel was "according to Matthew", even though it might contain sentences which were not written by Matthew at all. As long as the incident or the teaching was in keeping with the main stream which he had established, it seemed perfectly all right to the early Church to include it under Matthew's name. Perhaps the nearest we can get to understanding this in modern times is to consider standard works of reference. We may possess *Crockford's Clerical Directory,* but we do not expect it to be compiled by a man called Crockford today. We may have a general work of reference called *Whitaker's Almanack*. We rely on the name Whitaker to give the work integrity and reliability, but we do not expect there to be a living Whitaker who wrote every word of this year's edition.

### THE RETENTIVE ORIENTAL MIND

What seems to have happened, and in this I think all Christian scholars agree, is that the first three evangelists wrote down what had previously been an oral tradition. This is no more than intelligent guesswork, but it seems likely that in the early days of the Christian community there was no need to write down the stories of what Jesus said and did, especially as many of them were apparently expecting his early personal return. But what is not a guess but a fact is the fantastic retentiveness of the oriental mind. Stories are told by word of mouth again and again, and no verbal deviation or embellishment is allowed. It is a phenomenon rather like that which children exhibit when they are very young and have their favourite bed-time story. It must not vary in the slightest detail from the familiar pattern. Strangely enough only this very year I have been in contact with a friend who worked for some twenty-five years in business in Malaya. He found to his astonishment that conversations of twenty years ago and more, could be recalled perfectly, mistakes, faulty pronunciations and all, even though he himself had forgotten everything but the merest outline of such talk. Now this I am told would have been true of the Mediterranean world, and to me it seems most likely that it is the recollection of certain gems of speech and actions of Jesus which the first three evangelists record. This would account for the loose chronology, for we are reading not history in the modern sense but events and sayings treasured and remembered over a generation.

If we accept that the evangelists, or at any rate the first three, wrote down various oral traditions which had been passed on with scrupulous accuracy over the years, we shall be spared many unnecessary headaches. Is it not reasonable to suppose that Jesus gave his teaching in slightly different forms on various occasions to differing groups of people and that these were separately remembered and cherished? Before the days of mass communication (and that is not long ago) the prophet, preacher or politician was bound to repeat his message again and again. What he said would be couched in compressed, intelligible and memorable terms, but no one need suppose that he always used precisely the same words with parrot-like precision.

It is probable that Jesus spoke in Aramaic (a popular form of Hebrew), and if this is so then the evangelists had the extremely difficult job of listening to slightly varying accounts of the same, or similar, incidents and then setting them down in the widely-understood Greek of the time. They were not reporters in the modern sense, nor were they preparing a statement for any court of law. They were simply setting down in writing what had till then been memorised and repeated by word of mouth. It is highly unlikely that we shall get any more information about the life and teaching of Jesus than we have already. In a sense this is tantalising; what would we not give for a full-scale biography of this extraordinary man? How immensely valuable would be accurate descriptions of all that he ever said, as well as a detailed account of the events of his life. Why, we may plaintively ask, are we left almost completely in the dark about the childhood and young manhood of Jesus? Why have we no information, (which would be regarded as essential in any modern biography) about the formative influences which produced such a matchless character? Why do we know almost nothing of the period between what we commonly call the resurrection and the ascension? What was it that the now risen Christ then taught to his followers about the "things pertaining to the kingdom", as Luke describes them with such maddening brevity in the first chapter of "The Acts"? The plain answer is that we do not know.

The discovery of many *papyri* written in the same kind of Greek as the New Testament has certainly illuminated our understanding of many words and expressions of that time. The Dead Sea Scrolls may well fill in more of our knowledge of Palestinian life of about the time of Jesus. But it is highly unlikely that the small esoteric group who copied and preserved the scrolls will shed any fresh light upon the actual historic life of Jesus or even, as some suggest, of John the Baptist.

### THE AUTHORITY OF JOHN'S GOSPEL

This is not the place to write at any length about the Fourth Gospel. It is different in style, in vocabulary and in "atmosphere". Instead of the true nature of Jesus being discovered in the course of his ministry it is asserted at the beginning. Almost the whole of the story is set in Jerusalem. There is little mention of the extensive healing ministry of mind and body which the first three evangelists record. Instead of short parables we have quite lengthy discourses. There are times (inevitably, since New Testament Greek did not use quotation marks), when we are not sure whether we are reading the remembered words of Jesus himself or the comment of the evangelist. Nevertheless the impact of the whole Gospel is, one is tempted to say, greater than the other three put together. The author plainly knew Jesus and had had time to think and meditate on the significance of the "Word becoming flesh". Whether he knew the existing Gospels we do not know, but I did not get the impression that John was writing a deliberate correction. The feeling is that a man of more maturity and deeper insight is giving his account. He is in effect saying 'This is how I saw and heard Jesus Christ and this is the significance of his coming to this earth'. The result is the portrait of a character in no way different from the sketches supplied by Matthew, Mark and Luke but carrying an even deeper authority.

Naturally I have read a good number of commentaries on John's Gospel, and I am fairly familiar with the difficulties of deciding who was the author. I also know of the hard task awaiting anyone who tries to fit this work into a "harmony" with the other Gospels. But I was not primarily concerned with this sort of thing. My work was to translate for, not to confuse, the modern reader.

### THE STRENGTH OF JESUS AS A MAN

What happened to me as the work progressed was that the figure of Jesus emerged more and more clearly, and in a way unexpectedly. Of course I had a deep respect, indeed a great reverence for the conventional Jesus Christ whom the Church worshipped. But I was not at all prepared for the *unconventional* man revealed in these terse Gospels. No one could possibly have invented such a person: this was no puppet-hero built out of the imaginations of adoring admirers. "This man Jesus" so briefly described, rang true, sometimes alarmingly true. I began to see now why the religious Establishment of those days wanted to get rid of him at all costs. He was sudden death to pride, pomposity and pretence.

This man could be moved with compassion and could be very gentle, but I could find no trace of the "Gentle-Jesus-meek-and-mild". He was quite terrifyingly tough, not in a Bulldog Drummond – James Bond sort of way, but in the sheer strength of a unified and utterly dedicated personality. He once (at least) walked unscathed through a murderous crowd. I have known a few, a very, very few, men who could do that. But then I find that this sheer strength was still his after hours of unspeakable agony in the garden of Gethsemane. Those who were sent to arrest him "fell back to the ground". Previous pious generations attribute this to some supernatural power. I don't believe this for a moment. Jesus was a man of such complete authority that he could remain in command of a situation even when the odds were heavily against him.

## JESUS IS MAN, NOT SUPERMAN

It was this strength of human character which struck me again and again. We are not being told of a superman but of someone supremely human. He could work so hard that his followers begged him to stop. Yet he was fast asleep aboard the little fishing-boat while the others did the rowing. He was awake and out praying in solitude while the others were asleep, yet there were times when he was tired. "Jesus, being wearied with his journey, sat down beside a well", records John. He touched the untouchable leper, he made friends with those who had lost their reputation and self-respect. He denounced in vitriolic words the leaders of so-called "religion". He spoke fearlessly to the violently insane. He wept in the presence of human sorrow. He also wept over Jerusalem because its people utterly failed to recognise God's Messiah when he taught and preached among them, and also because with the true prophet's insight he foresaw the city's hideous destruction. Even with a little imaginative sympathy one could sense the agony of his frustration and near-despair. For the first time it seemed to me that it was because he was a human being almost at the end of his tether that this man cursed a fig tree, and then in the garden called for swords instead of cloaks. He admitted that he was terrified as he went into the garden of Gethsemane and he sweated there in fear and anguish.

The record of the behaviour of Jesus on the way to the cross and of the crucifixion itself is almost unbearable, chiefly because it is so intensely *human*. If, as I believe, this was indeed God focused in a human being, we can see for ourselves that here is no play-acting, this is the real thing. There are no supernatural advantages for this man. No celestial rescue-party delivered him from the power of evil men, and his agony was not mitigated by any superhuman anaesthetic. We can only guess what frightful anguish of mind and spirit wrung from him the terrible words, "My God, my God, why has thou forsaken me?"* But the cry "It is finished!" cannot be one of despair. It does not even mean "it is all over". It means "It had been completed" – and the terrifying task of doing God's will to the bitter end had been fully and finally accomplished.

### THE EMERGENCE OF A REAL PERSON

Here in the four Gospels, fragmentary as they sometimes are, emerges a real man, whose perfect integrity is compelling. He "spoke with authority", and "the common people heard him gladly" and even at the end of his public career those who were sent to arrest him returned empty-handed. "Never man spake like this man", was their comment.

But it would be a profound mistake to think that Jesus was merely an eloquent field-preacher who had got on the wrong side of authority. His character was strange and unpredictable. He was meek in the way that only the strong can truly be, yet he called, demanded and com-

* Or "My God, my God, why didst thou forsake me?" Both the Greek and the Hebrew of Psalm 22 (which is being quoted) would bear this translation.

manded without explanation or apology. What other man could call some fishermen to leave their skilled job, or ask somebody else to give up the lucrative, even though despised, work of tax-collecting and to follow him, and succeed? What other man could look straight at a ring of hostile faces and throw out the challenge "Which of you convinces me of sin?" and yet give no impression of arrogance or self-righteousness?

### JESUS' CHARACTER IS UNIQUE

Yet the flashes of light upon this character which the four Gospels reveal are often surprising. Jesus was not some penniless ascetic like John the Baptist before him. Luke records that there were many women who "ministered to him of their substance". We may be pretty sure that the house of Mary and Martha was not the only home where he could find rest and refreshment. His cloak, "woven without seam", was hardly the covering of a beggar. There can be no doubt that he was socially popular, and although we can discount the jibe that he was "a gluttonous man and a wine-bibber" we can fairly infer that he enjoyed God's good gifts of food and wine.

It struck me again and again that some of the unexpected sayings and actions of Jesus were recorded just because they were unexpected. The routine work (if we might so describe it) is sometimes dismissed in a few words – "he went about doing good and healing all manner of sickness and disease among the people". But the other words and works, which no one could have anticipated and which must have been nearly inexplicable at the time, are treasured and remembered with the utmost fidelity.

Yet woe betide any man who tries to fit this man into any
political or humanitarian slot! Those pacifists who would
claim him as their champion would do well to remember
that it was a soldier, a Roman commissioned officer, who
most evoked the admiration of Jesus. The parable of the
talents is enough to show that Jesus recognised the fundamental *inequality* of men in ability and possessions. The
stories of Jesus abound in such inequalities, in the difference between master and man, hard-working and lazy,
prudent and improvident. It is true that he denounced
hypocrisy, exploitation and lack of compassion. But he
made no attempt, as probably Judas Iscariot hoped, to
make himself a national champion. The "other-worldly"
aspect of his teaching cannot be fairly ignored. "My
kingdom" he insisted, "is not of this world." Yet it had
already "come upon men unawares" and was even then
"among" or "within" them. The way men treated one
another in this world was of paramount importance, but
Jesus recognised the obvious unfairness and injustice in
the here-and-now. In the end justice would be done and
be seen to be done, but not in this time-and-space world.
Jesus was no sentimental do-gooder and he spoke quite
unequivocally about rewards and punishments "in the
world to come." He declared that a man who harmed
one of his "little ones" would be better off dead. Some
of the most terrifying words ever written in the New
Testament are put into the mouth of Jesus. Yet they are
not threats or menaces but warnings given in deadly
earnest by the incarnation of unsentimental love.

What I am concerned with here is not to write a new
life of Jesus, but to set down my witness to the continued
shocks which his words and deeds gave me as I approached

68

the Gospels uninsulated by the familiar cover of beautiful language. The figure who emerged is quite unlike the Jesus of conventional piety, and even more unlike that imagined hero whom members of various causes claim as their champion. What we are so often confronted with today is a "processed" Jesus. Every element that we feel is not consonant with our "image" of him is removed, and the result is more insipid and unsatisfying than the worst of processed food.

## SOME WORDS ABOUT MIRACLES

A "miracle" is, by definition, something to be wondered at, and in the past, when laws then unknown were being used, it was commonly assumed that divine intervention was the cause of the wonder. People thought that God was somehow "interfering" with the working of Nature. I do not regard such an action as "impossible" (who are we to say what is "possible" and what is "impossible"?), but I think that it is unlikely. The vast and patient labours of all kinds of scientists reveal a consistency of natural order, but at the same time they discover complex laws which mankind never knew before. A distinguished professor of Physics and Chemistry who is a Fellow of the Royal Society, once said to me, "we labour for years to unlock one door, only to discover that we are confronted with six more locked ones!" I have met a few other really distinguished scientists in one field or another and each has said, in effect, "how little we know". It seems to me, therefore, just plain stupid to say that this or that is "impossible", however simply or naïvely it may be described.

Part of our modern *malaise* is that we are suffering from a surfeit of what would have been "miracles" only a century or so ago. We take them for granted, even though we do not know how they work. But if some marvel of healing is recorded in the New Testament, for instance, modern man writes it off at once as folk-lore! By what right do they do that? I would like some of our "modern" New Testament scholars who scoff at "miracles" to study the incredible ingenuity as well as the natural laws that lie behind the everyday electric equipment we use every day. There is often a terrifying arrogance which dismisses the fruit of years of labour, experiment and experience as "gadgets" and "contraptions". It may well be that I am fortunate, but it so happens that "radio" and sound reproduction have been my hobby since my school days. I could "make" (and that means only connect together the components of) a television set. But to understand the principles that lie behind modern electonic circuitry increases my sense of wonder rather than reduces it. Men are discovering almost every day some new law of Nature, which has been there all the time. Less than a century ago not only radio, radar and television but even such everyday objects of use as electric light and the telephone would have been completely unknown to the vast majority of people. If men and women of the early 1800's had suddenly been shown a television screen which was showing a picture of an event taking place (via a man-made satellite) three thousand miles away they would without doubt have called it a miracle (as indeed it is). But the laws which make the feat of skill and ingenuity a visible and audible experience have been there for countless aeons of time. There are literally thousands of such "miracles" in various departments of human life today. To me, even where I understand and can apply the principles, I retain my sense of wonder. But I cannot for the life of me understand those who automatically rule out the "miracles" of the Gospels.

### JESUS AND MIRACLES

I have already mentioned that in the process of translation a definite and indeed authoritative human character emerged from the combined writings of the evangelists. This man Jesus was much more of a human being than I had previously thought. I suppose that somewhere in the recesses of my mind I had stored a mixed-up impression of a being of supernatural perfection and certain supernatural powers. I believed, and indeed still do believe, that Jesus was both God and man. But the conclusion grew upon me that the Jesus of the Gospels really *was* man, not a demi-god and certainly not God playing, however convincingly, the part of man. I have written of the mental and spiritual toughness which co-existed in Jesus with extraordinary sympathy and compassion. So that when I came to the "miracles" of the Gospels I did not find in them anything incompatible with his character or his declared mission. They did not give me the impression of being celestial conjuring-tricks designed to produce faith. Indeed the records insist that Jesus did not want publicity for his acts of physical or mental healing. I think it is difficult for us today to appreciate the spiritual power of a man uniquely integrated and dedicated, and who spent many hours in solitary communion with God. The sense grew upon me with the years that such a man, so toughened and disciplined in following the path laid out for him by his Father, might quite easily possess

71

qualities of insight into the cause of a man's sickness, as well as the power to make him whole. Again, we need not quarrel with the picture-language. To those who saw the outward manifestations of an epileptic or some mental disorder which made a man violently destructive, it was not unnatural to think of him as possessing or being possessed by "a devil". Indeed those of us who have ever been in the presence of the violently deranged and looked into their eyes could easily agree that some evil power appears to be possessing the patient. It seems that Jesus was in many cases able to get to the storm-centre of the disturbance and resolve it with authoritative love. We do not know even yet how far the mind affects the body or the body the mind, or how far either of them is influenced by spiritual power – by intercessory prayer, for example. We know how to "cure" certain diseases with fair accuracy, but what we are really doing is removing the obstacles which are preventing a natural ability to heal itself which both the human body and mind possess. It does not seem to me in the least unreasonable that a man of concentrated spiritual power should be able to remove these obstacles instantaneously. The whole business of "spiritual" healing is a much debated one, and I do not propose to enter any controversy here. I am simply concerned to record my own conviction that the miracles of healing which Jesus performed were perfectly genuine, even though they may be described in the jargon of the day.

### FACT AND THE LANGUAGE OF REPORTING IT

This brings me to another important point. What we read in the Gospels is, I believe, true, but it is not necessarily described in words which we should use today, nearly two thousand years afterwards. A simple example springs to mind. In the three hours of darkness which fell over the whole countryside at the crucifixion of Jesus, Luke says that the sun's light failed, using the very Greek word which we use when we talk about an "eclipse". Luke gives me the impression of being a very careful writer who, to use our modern phrase, would "interview" people about what they remembered of the life and teaching of Jesus. Now *we* know that there could not have been an eclipse of the sun because that cannot happen at the time of the full moon, which was when Jesus died. We do not know whether Luke himself knew this. But since he records the failure of the sun's light and goes on to describe the dismay and confusion it caused (for men had no means of telling that the unnatural event was to last no more than three hours) it is perfectly possible that an eye-witness of that eerie darkness at noon might well have described it to Luke as an eclipse of the sun. We may never know in this life the cause of the phenomenon, but I believe that it happened and as a Christian I believe it to be a singularly impressive reflection in the natural world of what was happening on the cross.

To me this applies to any of the "miracles" of Jesus. Whether we one day know the laws of the spiritual sphere in which he was moving or not, I believe that the evangelists were setting down in terms of their own time what they actually observed. I am not therefore particularly worried when Mark reports that at the baptism of Jesus he (Jesus) "saw the heavens split open, and the Spirit coming down upon him like a dove. A voice came out of Heaven, saying, 'You are my dearly-beloved Son, in whom I am well pleased!'" (Mark 1: 10, 11) Whether Jesus alone saw this sight and heard these words, and later told his disciples about the occurrence, or whether

73

there were those of sufficient spiritual perception to see and hear what happened I do not know. For myself I believe it happened, but whether I should have heard any voice or seen anything beyond a flash of light is naturally open to question. It is very interesting to find that in John's Gospel where a "voice from heaven" speaks to Jesus shortly before his suffering and death, John records "When the crowd of bystanders heard this, they said it thundered, but some of them said, 'An angel spoke to him.' " (John 12: 29) What, then, I am concerned about is my conviction that many extraordinary events accompanied the life of Jesus but they are necessarily described in the language of those who were eye-witnesses.

LIGHT AND DARKNESS

There is a good deal in the New Testament about light and darkness, and I think we should constantly remind ourselves to what an extent we take artificial light for granted. Most of us live within touch of an electric light switch, many of us live in cities and towns whose streets and houses are illuminated, and the electric torch operated by a battery is a commonplace almost all over the world. We thus find in the world of the first century A.D. that light creates a much greater impression of divine presence or divine happening than speed or size or physical power, which are the things which impress many of us today. The story of the transfiguration is a particularly good example of this. The dazzling brightness of both the face of Jesus and his clothes filled Peter, James and John with exalted awe. I find this story interesting for another reason. Peter, James and John described what they saw and they observed Moses and Elijah talking to Jesus. It seems to me it would be quite possible to relate the incident in a different way. Suppose that the limitations of time and earthly life were, so to speak, momentarily lifted. Peter, James and John would then see Jesus radiantly bright talking without the slightest sense of anachronism with the two men of the past who represented the law and the prophets. Thus one could say not so much that Jesus was transfigured but that the disciples were temporarily relieved of their earth-blindness. It must have been an ecstatic experience and one which Peter, quite understandably, but in a rather clumsy way, wanted to prolong. Once again to me it bears the hall-mark of a true happening, however shortly and naïvely described.

### THE QUESTION OF PROPHECY

Closely allied to the miraculous elements in the life of Jesus is the authentic note of prophecy. Most people who know the Bible at all know that prophecy does not necessarily mean foretelling the future, although it may well include it. I have so far only made one excursion into the world of the Old Testament,* but a close study of the prophets' message shows that such men are primarily concerned to declare the "word of the Lord". They saw, sometimes with startling and heart-breaking clarity, what would be bound to happen if the nation continued on a course contrary to the will of the Lord. The time-sense was temporarily suspended, there is a dramatic "fore-shortening" of things which were to come. More frequently than not their vision was quite astonishingly accurate, even though twenty or a hundred years might elapse before what they foresaw came true. Their messages were "early warnings" rather than long-term

* *Four Prophets* (Bles).

75

threats. Prophecy is not necessarily prediction. For the warning contained in the vision might lead to a change of heart, and therefore of subsequent events.

I found this same prophetic note in the teaching of Jesus as recorded by the first three evangelists. At first I was tempted to think that various warnings of persecution and trouble in the future made by Jesus at different times had been put together by some first century Christian Jew into the accepted apocalyptic* form. Certainly there is a marked change of key; Jesus is not now giving definite teaching or even speaking in parables, he is speaking as the prophets spoke. He was, of course, on intimate terms with the prophetic writings of the Old Testament, and he must have known the special form in which much of that prophecy is set. So I came to change my view, and I believe now that there were times when Jesus, probably to the inner circle of the disciples, shared his insights about the future in the prophetic idiom which they would to some extent understand. He knew that terrible persecutions would follow his death, he could foresee the wars and famines, the terrible sufferings which were to befall humanity. He could see "men's hearts failing them for fear" as they saw the inevitable approach of terrible destruction. He also spoke of his own "coming" as being as unexpected as a thief in the night but as unmistakeably conspicuous as a flash of lightning. He spoke of himself as "coming" to judge the world. He wondered whether there would still be "faith" in the world when he should finally come. He knew how men's faith in God can be eroded by the anxieties and the many apparent injustices as well as by the present prosperity of evil. "Because iniquity shall abound the love of many shall wax cold." (Matt: 24,12).

* This word means "revealing", but prophets "revealed" divine truth often in picture-language which is puzzling to us.

"Eschatology" is the doctrine or teaching about "the last things" – death, judgment, heaven and hell. Much of today's Christianity is almost completely earthbound, and the words of Jesus about what follows this life are scarcely studied at all. This, I believe, is partly due to man's enormous technical successes which make him feel master of the human situation. But it is also partly due to our scholars and experts. By the time they have finished with their dissection of the New Testament and with their explaining away as "myth" all that they find disquieting or unacceptable to the modern mind, the Christian way of life is little more than humanism with a slight tinge of religion. For it is not only advertisers who attempt to deaden our critical faculties by clever words, there are New Testament scholars who, whether consciously or not, do the same thing. Thus, if you are to be thought up-to-date and "with it" you are expected to believe in current phrases. One of these is "realised eschatology", which means that all those things which Jesus foretold have happened, either at the destruction of Jerusalem in A.D. 70 or in the persecutions of the Church. In other words the prophetic element in the teaching of Jesus is of no value at all to us in the twentieth century. Such a judgment makes Jesus less of a prophet than Amos, Isaiah, Micah, Jeremiah and the rest. I find myself quite unable to accept this. There *is* an element of the prophecy of Jerusalem's terrible downfall and of the desecration of the Temple – the horror of which we who are not Jews find hard to appreciate. But the prophetic vision goes far beyond this. It envisages the end of the life of humanity on this planet, when, so to speak, eternity irrupts into time. There is no time-scale: there is rarely such an earthbound factor in prophetic vision. The prophet sees the truth in compelling terms, but he cannot tell the day or the hour of any event, still less the time of the final end of the whole human affair.

We are ourselves somewhere in the vast world-wide vision which Jesus foresaw, and, for all we know, we may be near the end of all things. You simply cannot read the New Testament fairly and come to the conclusion that the world is going to become better and better, happier and happier, until at last God congratulates mankind on the splendid job they have made of it! Quite the contrary is true; not only Jesus, but Paul, Peter, John and the rest never seriously considered human perfectibility in the short span of earthly life. This is the preparation, the training-ground, the place where God begins his work of making us into what he wants us to be. But it is not our home. We are warned again and again not to value this world as a permanency. Neither our security nor our true wealth is rooted in this passing life. We are strangers and pilgrims and while we are under the pressure of love to do all that we can to help our fellows, we should not expect a world which is largely God-resisting to become some earthly paradise. All this may sound unbearably old-fashioned, but this is the view of the New Testament as a whole.

In a true and real sense the Kingdom of God was already established upon earth, but none of the New Testament writers expects the vast work of redeeming the whole world to take place either easily or quickly.

Some of the early Christians, at least, apparently expected the return of their risen Lord in power in a very short time, and both Peter and Paul had to remind their converts that the "time" was entirely a matter of God's choosing. Meanwhile the Christian life must be led with

78

patience and courage, the true Gospel must be proclaimed and Christian worship continued. The light must shine in a dark and cruel world.

## THE CHRISTIAN PARADOX

It might be thought that if a man's hope and treasure lay in another, unseen world, he would have little contact with, or interest in, the world in which he is only a temporary resident. Of course there have been, and are, sects who live apart from the world, but that is not the general picture. It is not usually the atheists and agnostics who are to be found fighting disease, ignorance and fear in the most dangerous and difficult parts of the world. And this is because the Christian faith, although inevitably rooted in "heaven" is incurably earthly. The seeds of this paradoxical attitude are scattered throughout the New Testament. "Religion" which does not express itself in compassion is a dead and indeed a dangerous thing. Yet the root of the relief of disease, the removal of ignorance and the teaching of faith lies in the love of God. We love because God first loved us.

I feel I must stress this point because we seem to live in an atmosphere of "either/or" whereas it is really a matter of "both/and". Certainly it is useless to preach a gospel of the soul's redemption to a starving man. But it is equally valueless (and the world around is full of examples) to make men affluent in this world and at the same time deprive him of any sense of God or of any meaningful life after death. Compassion and charity are both popular words today, while faith in God is regarded as largely irrelevant. But in fact both compassion and charity can be monstrously misused unless they are informed by the love of God. Hence we get situations in which compassion goes out to the violent thug who assaults an old lady for her meagre savings, but none at all to her! Charity means instant social acceptance for the adulterer but little compassion for his deceived and deprived wife. To love God is the first and greatest commandment, said Jesus, and this is the priority insisted on throughout the New Testament.

### THE VALUE OF LUKE'S EVIDENCE

Strangely enough it was while translating that vibrant book commonly known as the Acts of the Apostles, and which I renamed *The Young Church in Action*, that the full weight of Christian evidence, centred as it must be in the resurrection, fell upon me with renewed force. But I must wait a little while before I expand this conviction. For the patient, careful Luke, with his sensitive "feeling" for words has more to tell us about Christian beginnings. I had already come to the conclusion that he was a careful historian, the kind of man who would tactfully but firmly persuade people to tell him what they had actually seen and heard, and check his information. We do not know exactly when Luke became a Christian. Apparently once he had embraced the Christian cause he became Paul's close companion in all kinds of danger and hardship. But, if the records are to be trusted and I believe they are, he was far more than "the beloved physician". He set himself out to write for Theophilus, a real or imaginary character, as true an account of the earthly life of Jesus as he could manage. When we come to his second work, the Acts, it is obvious that he has been asking further questions of eye-witnesses of events which he himself had not seen. Thus, in the opening chapter of Luke's second book, we get a more detailed and expanded version of what we commonly call the ascension. Here I think the picture has been spoiled for us by some literal-minded people who confuse the noisy, wasteful and expensive business of blasting a man into "space" with the quiet simplicity of the real acted parable of the ascension. There is no connection between the two; you might just as profitably enquire about the actual candlepower used in the transfiguration or of the light-intensity, brighter than the noon-day sun, which halted Saul in his tracks on his way to Damascus.

### THE ASCENSION WAS OBSERVED

I know it takes a little time for human minds to assimilate a stupendous new truth. Thus we find Jesus appearing and disappearing over a period of some six weeks. During this time he is not only teaching his disciples, but helping them to grow accustomed to the idea that he is *with* them, and indeed will be *in* them, whether he is visible or not. But eventually the time comes when he must show them as directly, simply and kindly as possible that as a bodily presence, such as they knew in the streets and on the hills of Palestine, he is to be no more with them. What could more plainly and finally convey to the men of those days this departure than the simple event of the ascension? There is no question of a "count-down" and a "blast-off"! In the act of blessing them the man, whom they knew and loved, rose there on the hill side until "a cloud received him out of their sight". This is what they saw, this is what they later reported to Luke, but it is not to be explained or explained away in terms of modern physics. Nevertheless it must have been an extraordinarily satisfying experience for these early disciples since they, according to Luke, "returned to Jerusalem with great joy". They knew now for certain that death had been conquered, they knew that their beloved Jesus was truly the Son of God, and ringing in their ears was the promise that they would be given the power to go out and to tell the world.

## THE YOUNG CHURCH BEGINS

I found Luke's account of the beginning of the young church strangely moving. This mere handful of early believers, who had deserted their Master the moment real danger threatened, and who had, apparently, taken so long to realise that he had really and demonstrably conquered death, are bidden to wait. They are convinced; they are full of joy. But they lack the power to breach the defences of an unbelieving world. The story, all too familiar to many of us who have been Christians for years, is told with extraordinary simplicity and economy of words. There must be some God-given power given to that tiny band, charged with the alarming (and seemingly impossible) task of "preaching the Gospel to every creature". And there was, for the living Spirit of God came upon these men in a way no one could have anticipated. Luke is describing, perhaps thirty years later, something of what men told him had happened at that momentous Pentecost. I cannot believe that Luke, or anybody else, concocted such a story. It is superhuman but not magical, and I find it wholly credible. There is this curious mixture of the earthly and the heavenly, which is typical of most of the New Testament. We have not gone very far in reading the Acts when, in chapter six, we come across a down-to-earth case of human grumbling, or possible jealousy. Whereupon seven more men are chosen as "deacons", among them Stephen, the first to suffer death for his faith. But even here Luke has an eye for a small but significant detail. In verse seven of the same chapter we read that "a great company of the priests were obedient to the faith". Frankly, I had never seriously considered this before. The established order of things ecclesiastical, which included "the priests", had always seemed to me to be the implacable enemies of Jesus, and later of Paul, wherever he travelled to proclaim the Gospel. Now I cannot believe that Luke made this up! It is one of those unexpected partial glimpses of truth which make the whole so convincing.

But as I continued to read Luke's fascinating story, I slowly realised that the message proclaimed was basically that of "Jesus and the Resurrection". (This was almost farcically true just before Paul preached, not altogether unsuccessfully, to the sermon-tasters on Mars Hill. Some Stoic and Epicurean philosophers thought he was proclaiming *two* "foreign deities", Jesus and Anastasis – resurrection!) The young church had, apparently no knowledge of what we nowadays call the Virgin Birth, or even of the Christmas Story. The great point to them was that God had become a human being, had been publicly executed, and then had *conquered death*. He had shown himself to them alive "by many infallible proofs" (Acts 1: 3) and had even eaten and drunk with them! (Acts 10: 41) Naturally they could never forget this, and, as the Gospel was preached to the then-known world, "Jesus the risen Lord" was the heart and core of their message. The resurrection of Jesus was, and indeed, is, historic fact. I suppose I have studied the relevant documents, commentaries and attempts to controvert the whole story as fully as most men, and I am utterly convinced that *this thing really happened*. I am deeply grateful to Luke for showing me that it was the resurrection from death of a man, God's chosen man, Jesus, which gave the early church its enormous drive, vitality, courage and hope.

This emphasis sent me back to re-study the Gospel records. Let us freely admit that the stories of the rising from the dead of the man Jesus are not mounted or arranged as evidence for any court of law – or for that matter for any critic. I should be highly suspicious of them if they were. People who are frightened and despairing, suddenly confronted with evidence which contradicts all their previous experience of life, can hardly be considered to be ideal witnesses. Wouldn't you be shaken to the marrow if a young man, whom you had seen die publicly and in agony on Friday, greeted you with a cheerful greeting on the following Sunday? Does it *matter* whether there was one "man in white" or two who spoke to the bewildered women at the opened sepulchre? Can we not understand that a woman half-crazy with grief and with eyes nearly blind with weeping should mistake a male figure in the early morning light for the gardener? Have we never been so overwhelmed with grief or disappointment, or both, that we literally do not *see* anything else? I am therefore not in the least worried by the story of the walk to Emmaus (recorded only by Luke, and possibly recovered by him in his patient researches). I see no difficulty in believing that the minds of Cleopas and his companion were so utterly preoccupied with the collapse of their hopes and dreams that they did not recognise Jesus. Obviously all the time that they had been walking with him their despair was melting and their faith in Jesus, God's Christ, was coming back to life. But the "psychological moment" came when they were relaxed at a friendly table, and a familiar gesture brought instant recognition. It all "clicked into place" as we say in modern slang or, as Luke records, "their eyes were opened and they knew him". Now no one makes up a story like this. They never have and they never will. This rings true; this certainly happened.

There is an almost haphazard recording of the appearances of Jesus after his resurrection, which I find extraordinarily convincing. I think my favourite again occurs in Luke's work. When the two who were walking to Emmaus had rushed back to Jerusalem to report their astounding experience to the eleven, they found that they already knew that "the Lord is risen indeed and hath appeared to Simon". Again, according to Luke, while they are still talking excitedly Jesus himself appears among them. They were, as we might say, scared out of their wits; they thought they were seeing a ghost. But Jesus reassures them and, as was his habit, he asks penetrating questions. "Why are you so worried?" "Why do doubts arise in your minds? Look at my hands and my feet – it is really I myself! Feel and see: ghosts have no flesh or bones as you can see that I have." Then Luke makes his shrewd comment as a doctor and student of human nature. Some things are too good to be true, and the human mind cannot accept them at once. It is entirely natural to me that Luke should record that "they still could not believe it through sheer joy and were quite bewildered". Then follows this extraordinary, and, in a way amusing test of whether Jesus really was there in person. He asks them, "Have you anything here to eat?" We can imagine the frantic dash to a shelf or cupboard where they kept their food, and we can imagine that they saw no incongruity in offering him a piece of broiled fish and part of a honeycomb. But I myself cannot imagine that Jesus consumed this rather strange meal before their eyes without a smile! But this in a way clinched it; whoever heard of a ghost *eating*? Again I find this is the kind of story which no man would invent, but which any man who was present would remember until his dying day. And Luke, bless him, records it.

John, writing considerably later, contents himself with remarking, "many other signs truly did Jesus in the presence of his disciples which are not written in this book". We cannot help wishing he had written more.

### THE RESURRECTION-BODY OF JESUS

Although it is clear that Jesus meant his friends to understand that he had truly conquered death, and sometimes went to great pains to convince them of the fact (see especially John 20: 27), even a cursory reading of the Gospel stories is enough to show that the "appearances" are not the same in quality. On some occasions Jesus, now the risen Christ, appears among his astonished disciples when they are met behind closed doors, and sometimes he appears in the open air. Apparently his visible presence could disappear instantly, yet apparently he could also make himself not only visible but tangible to human senses. In the earliest account of the resurrection appearances, which Paul records in 1 Cor. 15, he seems to make no distinction between the different kinds of appearance. His own vision of the risen Lord is to him as valid as the experience of the Apostles, "the five hundred brethren assembled at once", and the others. Nevertheless I am pretty certain that, if pressed, Paul would be the first to admit that the appearances were different in kind. The important thing to him was that "this man Jesus" had been "raised" by God from the dead, and had been set above all power in heaven and earth.

## THE IMPORTANCE OF THE EMPTY TOMB

It does not worry me in the least that the man whom God had proved to be his Christ, and to whom he had given "all power in heaven and in earth" should use his "resurrection-body" in any way that he chose. There are such things as visions and there are hallucinations, but the more I study the evidence the more I am convinced that Jesus was raised from the dead, body and all, in a real sense, leaving an open tomb and empty grave-clothes. I still think Frank Morison's book *Who Moved the Stone*\* well worth serious attention. I am wholeheartedly in agreement with Mary Essberger who wrote in the *Church Times* last Easter:

"Can Dr. Lampe please explain convincingly why Caiaphas and the priestly conclave did not simply march down to the grave, break the seals, and have a three-day exhibition of the mortal remains – proceeds from the viewing to be in aid of Temple funds, naturally! Can he explain why the trained hardened soldiers suddenly deserted their post and dashed back to face what might have been court-martial and execution? Or why they were bribed to spread an obviously false story when the simple remedy would have been to march them back, under escort, prove them wrong, and have them beheaded on the spot as a warning to any who might have fancy, super-natural ideas?

"Can he also explain the behaviour of Caiaphas and

\*Faber (paperback).

the priestly clique, which was so psychologically out-of-character? Quite honestly, had I been Caiaphas and *found* an empty tomb, I'd have produced a 'body' – any body – rather than let them get away with it and cause more havoc. That is, unless I, too, were suffering from some psychological shock amounting to a form of mental paralysis. That they did not do this is in itself something of a psychological phenomenon which needs as much investigating as the Resurrection itself. Men of that religio-political calibre would be prevented from such a 'cover-up' only by some inner uncertainty and confusion, some form of shock and paralysis stemming from a real though unvoiced fear, or else by the fact that too many people, even amongst their own number, had seen the empty tomb to make it safe to play any tricks.

"Through history the fact has remained that no body was ever produced (which would have been the simplest thing in the world to do *if there were a body available*) . . .

"Perhaps the simple answer is too simple . . . Perhaps there was no body to produce, and the Ascension is merely the logical 'follow-on' of that incredible (and, to some people, highly uncomfortable) fact of the Resurrection of the Man-God, Jesus Christ."

### SOME PERSONAL EXPERIENCE

Let me say at once that I am incredulous by nature, and as unsuperstitious as they come. I have never bothered about the number thirteen, or walking under ladders (making sure, of course, that there isn't a man with a paint-pot just above my head), or any of the current superstitions which may occupy the human heart in the absence of faith. Indeed, I laugh like the proverbial drain when the predictions of celebrated clairvoyants turn out to be false, as they mostly do. Anyone can make predictions which are so vague that they are meaningless to any intelligent reader, yet most of the popular press still give space to "What the Stars Foretell". The late *Picture Post* demonstrated this absurd nonsense of combined astrology and so-called clairvoyance shortly before World War II. All the stars, and nearly all the clairvoyants had predicted that there would not be a war. But there was! I mention this because I am not the sort of person who is readily taken in by the fraud and the plausible liar. Experience as Vicar of a parish soon cures you of this if nothing else will! But from time to time in life strange things occur which convince me that "there are more things in heaven and earth", John Robinson and friends, "than are dreamt of in your philosophy". I have had first-hand incontrovertible experience of extra-sensory perception, and a little of precognition. But the experience I want to mention here is relevant to the matter of the resurrection.

Many of us who believe in what is technically known as the Communion of Saints, must have experienced the sense of nearness, for a fairly short time, of those whom we love soon after they have died. This has certainly happened to me several times. But the late C. S. Lewis, whom I did not know very well, and had only seen in the flesh once, but with whom I had corresponded a fair amount, gave me an unusual experience. A few days after his death, while I was watching television, he "appeared" sitting in a chair within a few feet of me, and spoke a few words which were particularly relevant to the difficult circumstances through which I was passing. He was ruddier in complexion than ever, grinning all over his face and, as the old-fashioned saying has it, positively glowing with health. The interesting thing to me was that I had not been thinking about him at all. I was neither alarmed nor surprised nor, to satisfy the Bishop of Woolwich, did I look up to see the hole in the ceiling that he might have made on arrival. He was just *there* – "large as life and twice as natural"! A week later, this time when I was in bed reading before going to sleep, he appeared again, even more rosily radiant than before, and repeated to me the same message, which was very important to me at the time. I was a little puzzled by this, and I mentioned it to a certain saintly Bishop who was then living in retirement here in Dorset. His reply was, "My dear J. . . ., this sort of thing is happening all the time".

The reason why I mention this personal and memorable experience is that although "Jack Lewis" was real in a certain sense it did not occur to me that I should reach out and touch him. It is possible that *some* of the appearances of the risen Jesus were of this nature, being known technically as veridical visions. But the writers of the Gospels in their naïve unselfconscious way make it plain that something much more awesome and indeed authoritative characterised Christ's "infallible proofs".

### THE REVOLUTION OF THE RESURRECTION

Even though the Gospels are not, as I have said, biographies, they build up a picture of a man whose stature and quality are unsurpassed in history. Yet no man rescued him from humiliation, mockery and a torturing death. No celestial rescue-party intervened. It was not merely the end of all their hopes and dreams to the early Christians, but a cruel outrage to their sense of justice. If ever there was a case for divine intervention surely it was here. Once, in a moment of inspiration, Simon Peter had said, "You are Christ, the Son of the living God!" And we may fairly assume that the others had come to share this view to a greater or less extent. Yet it was not to a band of expectant hero-worshippers that Jesus appeared, but to men and women stunned by bitter grief and shattering disappointment. We can only guess at the black cloud of disillusionment which must have swept over them. After this terrible, final and public disaster they had, apparently, forgotten that he himself had foreseen and indeed forewarned them of what would happen.

It was against a background of broken hope and utter despair that the great miracle occurred. All four evangelists spend quite a lot of their short narratives in recounting the betrayal, the mock-trial, the final humiliations and the criminal execution. I do not think this was done merely for dramatic effect. It was written to show what even the best of men could suffer in this evil world. It was written to show all who should follow Jesus that he was not God *pretending* to be a man, but God who had become a man.

Thus the resounding triumph of the resurrection was all the more splendid and magnificent. Armed with no supernatural equipment Jesus had conquered man's last enemy, death. He had shown beyond any possible doubt that the victory was complete. To live again was no longer a pious hope or a wishful thought; it was a certainty. No conspiracy, no trick, no hysterical vision was responsible for this new certainty. As Paul remarked crisply some years later to King Agrippa, "this thing was not done in a corner". (Acts 26: 26)

I believe it to be very important indeed that close examination of the New Testament should produce conviction of its truth. No one is going to take the trouble to read it if once the idea becomes accepted that all we have is a collection of myths – and that is what is suggested by some of our so-called experts. Thus the Christian Church (and by that I mean all the Churches) is regarded by many as a collection of people blindly clinging to beliefs which everyone else knows are false and refusing to meet modern scientific truth. Obviously there are some Christians who are obscurantists in their outlook, but I have met a good many of most denominations both here and in America who are displaying the same Christian qualities as the people described in the New Testament. They are refusing to be secularised and they are refusing to allow the State or humanism or anything else to occupy the place which belongs to God.

Naturally we cannot turn the clock back, and it would be stupid to pretend that life anywhere in today's world is the same as the life of New Testament times. But people are the same, and the basic problems of human relationships are the same. The Spirit which Jesus promised would lead his followers "into all truth" is very actively at work wherever he is allowed. Some of his work is painful in the extreme. There has often to be the breaking-up of old ways of thinking, the expansion of responsibility and the checking of priorities. Any one who opens his personality to the living Spirit takes a risk of being considerably shaken. It seems obvious to me that the Churches themselves are also being shaken, perhaps as they have not been for centuries.

But we need not fear. The Spirit of truth does not

contradict himself. It is not that the essential faith revealed in the New Testament is shown to be wrong; it is much more that our eyes are opened and we see how much more deeply relevant that faith is to our modern days than we thought. So that we do not gain but lose if we dismiss what was written by the inspiration of the same Spirit as folk-tale or myth. He will certainly lead us into all truth, but he will not lead us into arrogance and a confusion between technical advance and spiritual wisdom. He will certainly help us to "communicate" the truth of God to other people, but he becomes our enemy the moment we attempt to modify the wisdom of God to fit the "cleverness" of the twentieth century. The stern words of Paul have a peculiar aptness to the modern situation when he says, "The foolishness of God is wiser than men". (1 Cor.1: 25)

. . .

This testimony to the essential truth of what the New Testament writers were inspired to say is mine. But I would like to quote two paragraphs from a recently published book called *The Life and Teaching of Jesus**  by Dr. William Neil of Nottingham University. The first is this:

"More and more it becomes clear that we are unlikely to get any answers that will satisfy the deepest needs of the human spirit from any other quarter" [i.e. than the Christian faith]. "Present day science and philosophy give us little help on the ultimate questions of human destiny. Social, political and educational panaceas leave most of us unpersuaded. If we are not to end our quest for truth about ourselves and the world we live in, in cynicism and disillusionment, where else can we turn but to religion?"

And the second is:

* Hodder and Stoughton.

"Organised Christianity is still in its infancy, as is the mind of man as he seeks to grapple with the truths that could only come to him by revelation. The half has not yet been told and the full implications for human thought and action of the coming of God in Christ have as yet been only dimly grasped by most of us."

Prejudiced? Of course I am prejudiced. Every one of us is, but at least, if we are adult and educated, we can be aware of our bias and make proper adjustment. I can only say that in translating the Greek of the New Testament into modern English I made every effort to correct any bias of which I was conscious. When I came to compare it with the writings which were excluded from the New Testament by the early "Fathers" I can only admire their wisdom. Probably most people have not had the opportunity to read the apocryphal "gospels" and "epistles", although every scholar has. I can only say here that in such writings we live in a world of magic and make-believe, of myth and fancy. In the whole task of translating the New Testament I never for one moment, however provoked and challenged I might be, felt that I was being swept away into a world of spookiness, witch-craft and magical powers such as abound in the books rejected from the New Testament. It was the sustained down-to-earth faith of the New Testament writers which conveyed to me that inexpressible sense of the genuine and the authentic.

Most of the clergy are not nearly so naïve as people may think and most of them have a pretty intimate knowledge of what human nature is like. Through years of experience they learn to distinguish the false from the true, the rogue and the impostor from the man who is in actual trouble and distress. This sense, which belongs to the expert in every field, is only partly intuitive. Most of it has to be learned in the hard school of experience. Thus we "of the cloth" learn to recognise the phoney begging letter, the bogus testimonial and the false front put up by men and women, so often in pathetic self-defence. This ability to discriminate does not desert us when we move into the field of what man has written. We acquire a "nose" for the fake and the imitation even though it may deceive the inexpert. It is my serious conclusion that we have here in the New Testament, words that bear the hall-mark of reality and the ring of truth.